Y0-CJC-673

GOD IS FOR YOU

He Is

HERE AND NOW

I Am

He Is I Am: God Is for You Here and Now

Copyright © 2025 Joel Osteen

All rights reserved. No part of this book may be reproduced or transmitted in any form or by any means, electronic or mechanical, including photocopying, recording, or by any information storage and retrieval system, without permission in writing from the publisher.

Scripture quotations marked AMP are taken from the Amplified® Bible (AMP), Copyright © 2015 by The Lockman Foundation. Used by permission. lockman.org

Scripture quotations marked BSB are taken from the Berean Study Bible®. Public domain.

Scripture quotations marked ESV are taken from The ESV® Bible (The Holy Bible, English Standard Version®), © 2001 by Crossway, a publishing ministry of Good News Publishers. Used by permission. All rights reserved.

Scripture quotations marked MSG are taken from *The Message*, copyright © 1993, 2002, 2018 by Eugene H. Peterson. Used by permission of NavPress. All rights reserved. Represented by Tyndale House Publishers.

Scripture quotations marked NASB are taken from the (NASB®) New American Standard Bible®, Copyright © 1960, 1971, 1977, 1995, 2020 by The Lockman Foundation. Used by permission. All rights reserved. lockman.org

Scripture quotations marked NIV are taken from the Holy Bible, New International Version®, NIV®. Copyright © 1973, 1978, 1984, 2011 by Biblica, Inc.™ Used by permission of Zondervan. All rights reserved worldwide. www.zondervan.com The "NIV" and "New International Version" are trademarks registered in the United States Patent and Trademark Office by Biblica, Inc.™

Scripture quotations marked NKJV are taken from the New King James Version®. Copyright © 1982 by Thomas Nelson. Used by permission. All rights reserved.

Scripture quotations marked NLT are taken from the *Holy Bible*, New Living Translation, copyright © 1996, 2004, 2015 by Tyndale House Foundation. Used by permission of Tyndale House Publishers, Carol Stream, Illinois 60188. All rights reserved.

ISBN: 978-1-963492-29-3

Created and assembled for Joel Osteen Ministries by
Breakfast for Seven
breakfastforseven.com

Printed in the United States of America.

For additional resources by Joel Osteen, visit JoelOsteen.com.

GOD IS FOR YOU

He Is

HERE AND NOW

I Am

JOEL OSTEEN

CONTENTS

A Note from Joel 1

Introduction 2

I Am the Bread of Life 8

I Am the Door 20

I Am the Light 34

I Am the Good Shepherd 48

I Am the Resurrection and the Life 64

I Am the Way, the Truth, and the Life 80

I Am the Vine 98

I Am the Alpha and the Omega 116

Am the Bread
I Am the Doo
Am the Light I A
e Good Shepherd
n the Resurrectio
d the Life I Am th
ay, the Truth, an
e Life I Am the Vi
Am the Alpha an
e Omega I Am th

A NOTE FROM JOEL

In the New Testament, Jesus emphasizes eight specific ways He wants to move in our lives. Each "I Am" is not just a statement but a promise that no matter what we face, Jesus is "here and now" for us. He is present, empowered, and eager to provide for us. He wants to be everything to us and is ready to fill our lives with His salvation, power, and provision in any given moment.

He is called the "Great I Am." The power of this truth lies in understanding that Jesus is not the "Great I Might," the "Great at Some Point," or the "Great Probably Not for You." He desires to work in your life now, right now. I encourage you to embrace these truths, grow in your faith, and experience the abundant life Jesus promises to those who follow Him.

Recognizing Jesus as the "I Am" means understanding that He is not just a historical figure but the living God actively involved in your life today. Be encouraged that as you trust in Jesus, you will find fulfillment in Him, embrace His salvation, live by His truth, and stay connected to Him as the true source of spiritual life . . . He is "I Am" in your life today, intimately and personally!

INTRODUCTION

In Exodus 3, God spoke to Moses at the burning bush, instructing him to go to Pharaoh and lead the Israelites out of Egypt. When Moses asked what name he should give to the people of Israel, God responded, *"I am who i am. Say this to the people of Israel: I am has sent me to you"* (Exodus 3:14, NLT).

When God told Moses, *"I am who i am,"* He revealed His eternal nature. The phrase "I Am" means that God exists outside of time — He has no beginning and no end. God has always been and always will be. This eternal existence sets Him apart as the one true God.

God was also conveying His self-sufficiency. He is not dependent on anything or anyone for His existence or power. Everything else in creation relies on something else to exist, but God is the source of all life and creation. By identifying Himself as "I Am," God declares He is the ultimate authority, the cause, and the foundation of all that exists.

The name also describes God's unchanging character. What He was in the past remains today, and He will be in the future. His nature, His promises, and His purposes are constant and reliable. In an ever-shifting and uncertain world, God's revelation as "I Am" reassures us of His steadfastness and faithfulness. He is — I Am for you here and now.

Finally, this name emphasizes God's personal presence. By using the phrase "I Am," God conveys His closeness to Moses and His people. He is not a distant, impersonal deity but an intimately involved God who is present with His people in their circumstances. It was a declaration that the God of Abraham, Isaac, and Jacob — the same God who had faithfully led their ancestors — was with Moses and would lead Israel out of Egypt.

John Saw Who He Was

Jesus used the same phrase "I Am" to describe Himself. John, the youngest disciple whom Jesus loved, had a close relationship with Jesus. He leaned on Jesus' chest, saw Him as his mentor and teacher, and likely had the closest bond with Him. John records these powerful declarations of who Jesus said He is. No other person had this revelation or insight into what Jesus described about Himself.

John's insight into the importance of these declarations likely stemmed from his close and intimate relationship with Jesus. Often referred to as the disciple whom Jesus loved, John had a deeper spiritual connection, allowing him to know the weight and meaning of Jesus' words in ways others may have missed.

While the other apostles may have witnessed these declarations, John was the one who recognized their theological and prophetic importance. These "I Am" statements were affirmations of Jesus' Messiahship and His equality with God. John understood that by claiming "I Am," Jesus fulfilled prophecies and directly identified Himself with Yahweh, the eternal, self-existent God.

Jesus later says, *"I tell you the truth, before Abraham was even born, I am!"* (John 8:58, NLT). Jesus is not only declaring His divinity but also His eternal nature. From the beginning, Jesus was with God, and He was God. Jesus declares He is more than just a prophet or teacher; He is God.

Jesus' Proclamations

Jesus declared that He is the One who satisfies our deepest hunger (the Bread of Life), the One who gives light to the world (the light), and through Him, salvation is available (the gate). He lays down His life for us (the Good Shepherd), the One who holds eternal life (the resurrection and the life), and the embodiment of truth (the way, the truth, and the life). Jesus also identified Himself as the source of spiritual vitality and fruitfulness (the true vine). Jesus fulfills Old Testament prophecies about the Messiah, predicts His resurrection, and presents Himself as the only way to salvation.

These statements are vital declarations of Jesus' identity and mission, each revealing a different aspect of His divine nature and relationship with us. Jesus' revelation of Himself to John tells us who He is, what He means to those who believe in Him, and what He has made available for us. These declarations give us key insights into who Jesus is and what He promised to be for us.

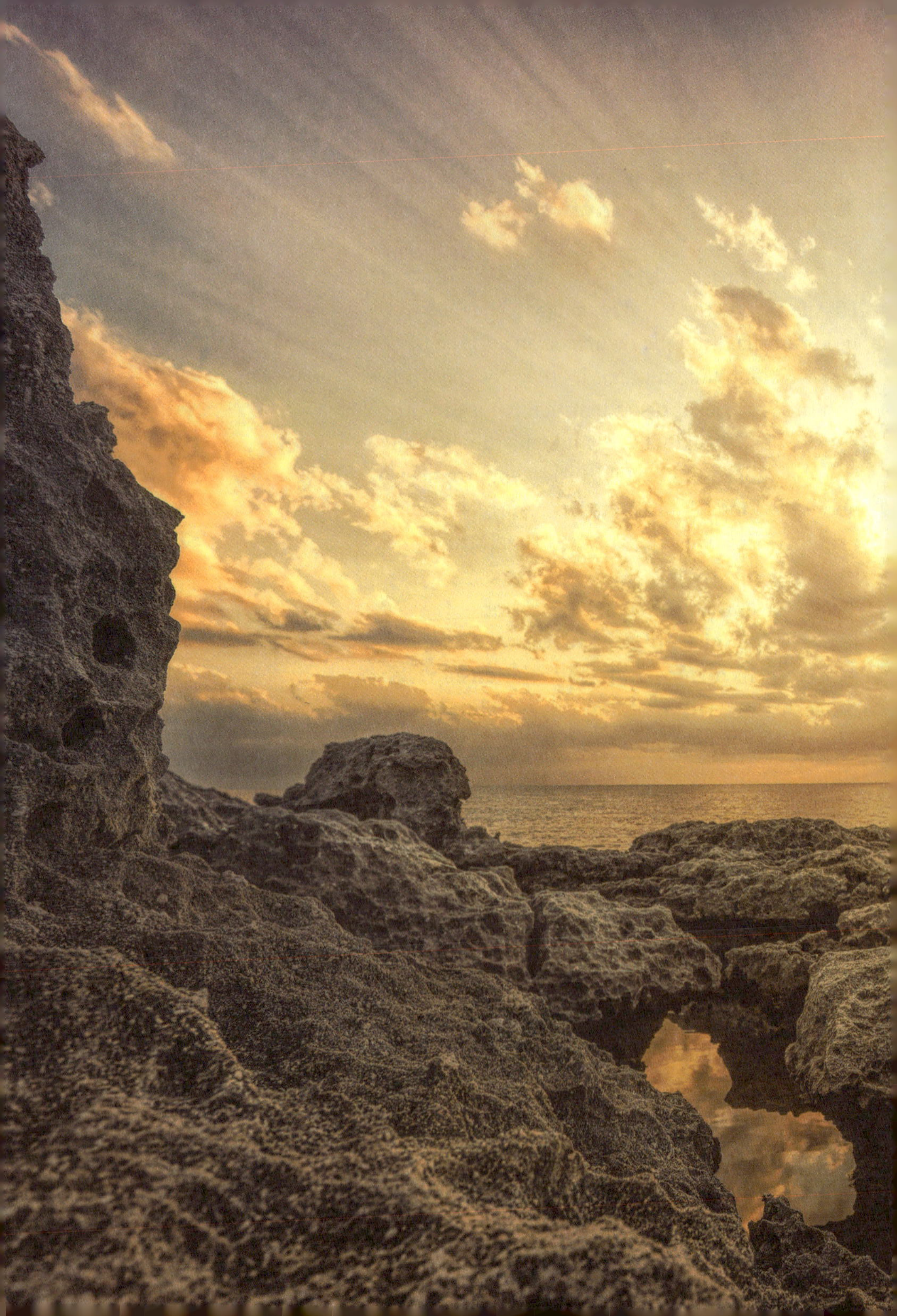

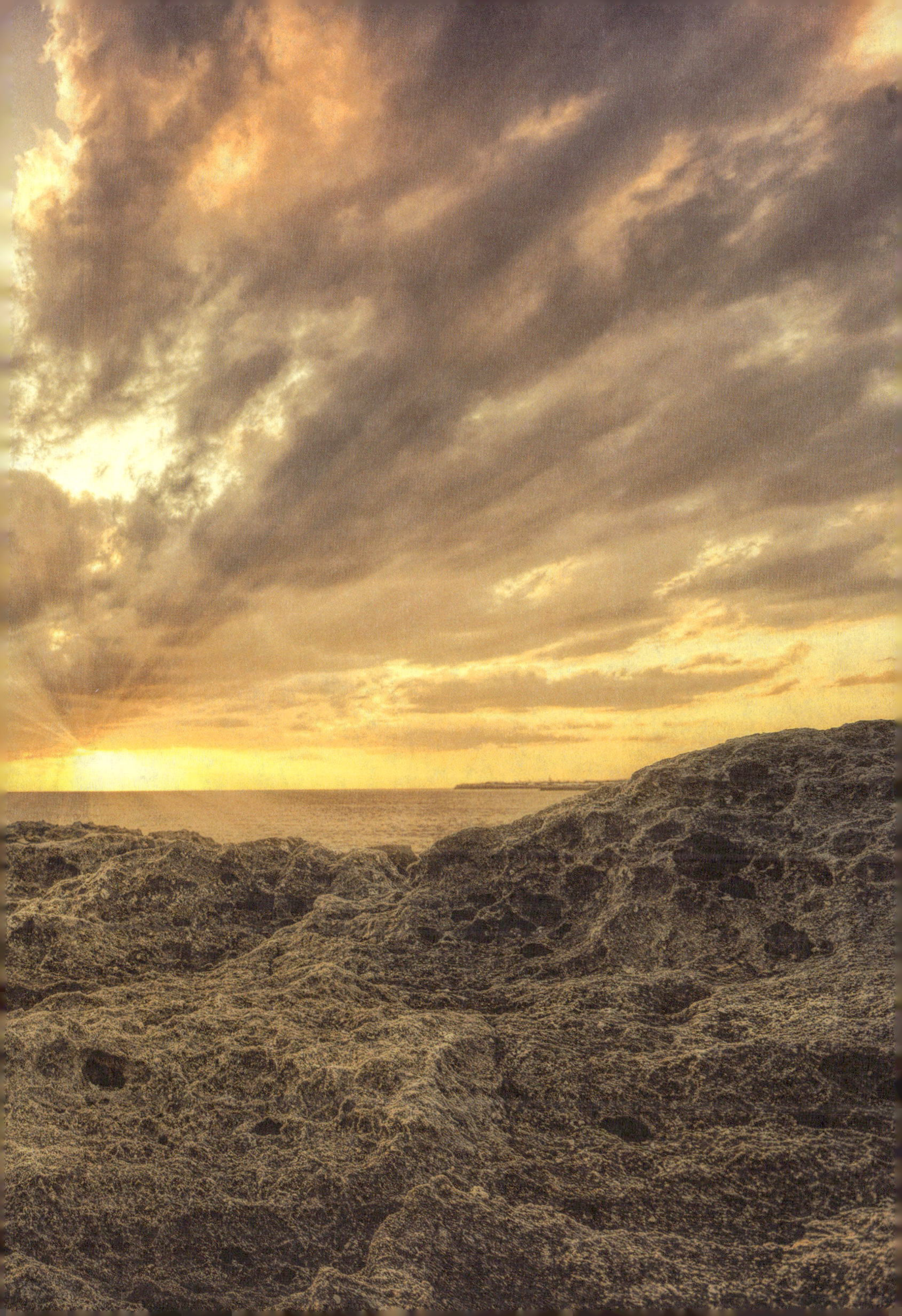

I Am the Bread of Life

Jesus replied, "I am the bread of life. Whoever comes to me will never be hungry again. Whoever believes in me will never be thirsty."

JOHN 6:35 (NLT)

I Am the Bread of Life

Just as bread nourishes the body, Jesus — the Bread of Life — nourishes your soul and satisfies your every need, whether physical, emotional, or spiritual. He provides the sustenance you require for fullness and wholeness in all aspects of life.

When Jesus calls Himself the Bread of Life, He's telling you that He is essential for your spiritual well-being. Just like you need food to nourish your body, you need Jesus to nourish your soul. He offers the spiritual strength, purpose, and fulfillment you long for, satisfying the deepest hunger in your heart.

With Jesus, your life becomes complete, as He cares for all your needs — spiritual, emotional, and even beyond what you can see. Without Him, true fulfillment is out of reach, but with Him, you can experience the fullness of life He offers.

A Broken Woman

A dejected and heartbroken woman meets a stranger at the watering hole. Her life is in turmoil — married five times and now living with a sixth man — she's faced rejection, heartache, and exploitation. Unlike others who come to the well in the cool of the morning or evening, she draws water at noon to avoid their judgment and harsh comments. Shame and embarrassment drive her to isolate herself.

She likely hung her head as she approached the well, feeling unworthy, ashamed, and devalued. Emotional wounds from broken relationships tormented her. She sought fulfillment through intimacy but remained empty, hungry, and unfulfilled.

As a young girl, she probably dreamed of a happy marriage and family, but life didn't turn out that way. She made mistakes; others wronged her. Now she was hurting, lonely, and bitter.

As the stranger approached, He asked for a drink. She was surprised — Jews avoided Samaritans, considering them impure, having intermarried with non-Jews. And in that culture, men didn't freely speak to women in public.

Yet Jesus broke the rules to reach her. He went against all social norms, against cultural expectations, to lift the fallen, heal the hurting, and restore the broken. The Bread of Life was about to change her life forever.

During their conversation, Jesus offered her "living water." He said, *"Those who drink the water I give will never be thirsty again. It becomes a fresh, bubbling spring within them, giving them eternal life"* (John 4:14, NLT). The living water He offered would quench and satisfy her deepest spiritual thirst.

Surprised, she asked, "Please, give me this water!" Her words revealed her belief that Jesus alone could satisfy her deepest longings.

Her encounter with Jesus that day transformed her from starving to satisfied. Overjoyed, she left her water jar and hurried back to town, telling everyone, *"Come, see a man who told me everything I ever did. Could this be the Messiah?"* (John 4:29, NIV).

Because of her testimony, many Samaritans believed in Jesus. Her encounter not only changed her life but also transformed her entire community. She came to the well ashamed, defeated, and broken. But she left with a new identity: valued, forgiven, redeemed. No longer looked down upon, she found respect and purpose. No longer broken, she saw herself as a child of the Most High.

Jesus explained that while physical food nourishes the body, spiritual food nourishes the soul (John 6:26–27). Jesus offers something eternal

PROMISE:
Many today have an inner hunger they can't satisfy. Jesus, the Bread of Life, promises to fill us completely.

— resurrection life, abundant life, and satisfaction that fulfills our deepest hunger.

Daily Bread

"Give us this day our daily bread."
MATTHEW 6:11 (NKJV)

Who doesn't love freshly baked bread straight from the oven? With or without butter, it's delicious. In the same way, our hunger for spiritual fulfillment is only truly satisfied by Jesus. He is enough — more than enough — to meet our deepest needs and longings.

Many people live unsatisfied and unfruitful lives because they lack nourishment. They need the Bread of Life — Jesus, who speaks life into their souls. Jesus said, *"Man shall not live by bread alone, but by every word that proceeds from the mouth of God"* (Matthew 4:4, NKJV). As we feast on His words, our souls will find nourishment and fulfillment. Jesus satisfies our deepest spiritual needs. Just as physical bread sustains the body, Jesus sustains the soul, offering lasting satisfaction.

Jesus said in Matthew 6:11, *"Give us this day our daily bread"* (ESV). He didn't say "our weekly bread" or "our monthly bread." It's not enough to just go to church on Sunday. Every morning, you need to go to God for your daily bread — your daily wisdom, direction, and strength. Too often, we try

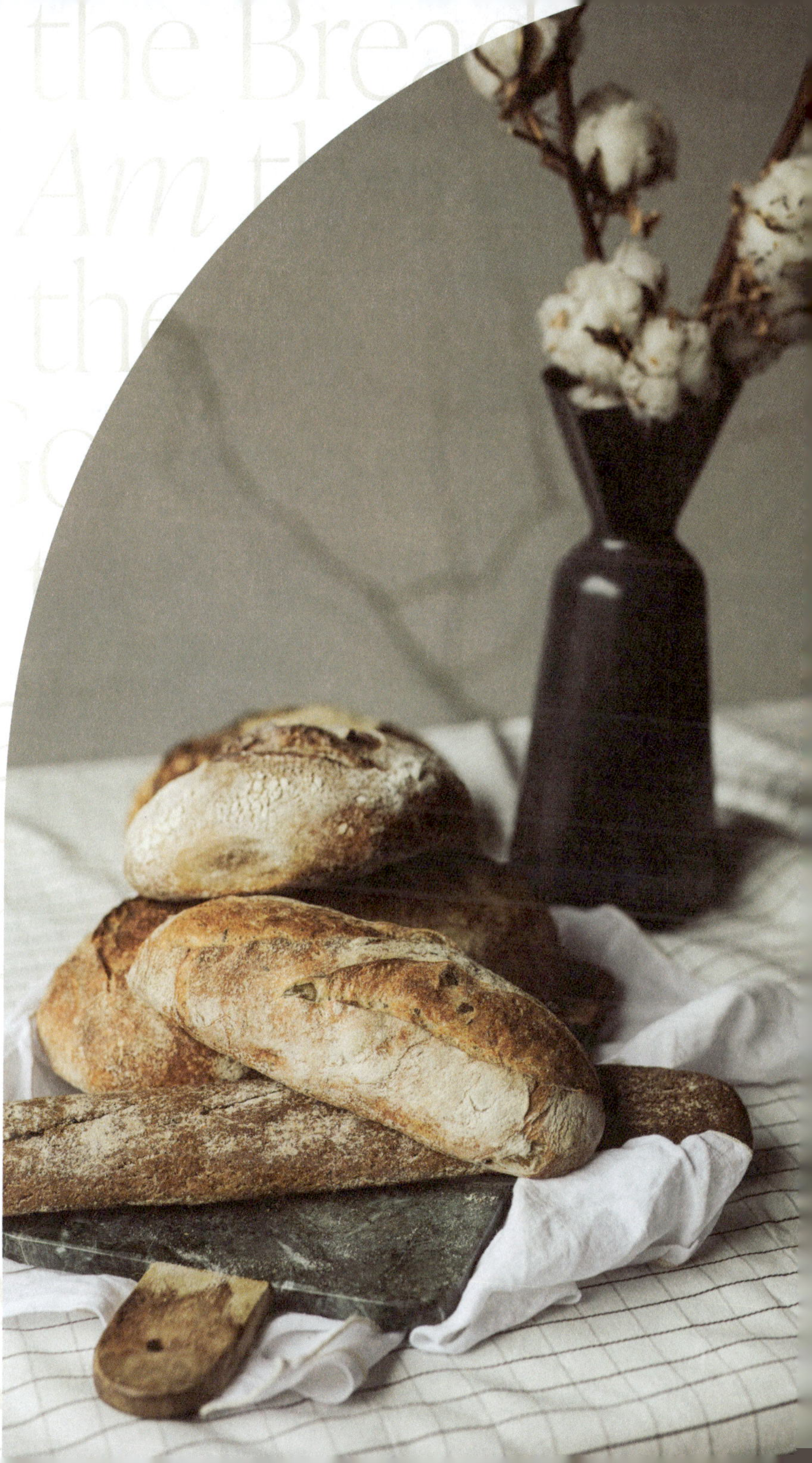

PROMISE:
You can overcome circumstances that rob you of Jesus' abundant, fulfilling life. Live the purposeful, joy-filled life that Jesus has purchased for you.

to handle things solely in our own strength, intellect, and ability, but that approach limits us.

God knows things we don't know. He sees what we can't. He knows the right people who should be in our lives, where danger lies, and where dead ends are. God knows how to catapult you years ahead, how to thrust you into your destiny. You have an advantage — are you taking time to get your daily bread?

Are you relying on past sources for your provision? Perhaps God is opening new paths, new streams of blessing, and new directions for healing. If you seek your daily bread in Him, listening to His voice, you'll experience spiritual life flowing in new and powerful ways.

Heaven's Bread

> *"I am the living bread that came down from heaven. Whoever eats this bread will live forever. This bread is my flesh, which I will give for the life of the world."*
> **JOHN 6:51 (NIV)**

When Jesus declared, *"I am the bread of life"* (John 6:35, NIV), He connected Himself with the miracle of manna. For forty years, God provided manna — bread from Heaven — to satisfy the Israelites' hunger in the wilderness. Every morning they had to go out and get a new supply.

I'm sure some people thought *I'm going to gather up enough for a whole week. I don't want to come tomorrow; I'll save time and energy; get it all done at once.* But they woke up the next day and the manna was all spoiled. You couldn't eat it. The principle being that every morning you had to go out and get fresh manna.

The word manna in Hebrew is translated, "What is it?" When we go to God each day for that fresh manna, the right attitude is, "God, what is it that You want me to do? What is my assignment?"

God wants us to come to Him for our daily bread. He's looking for people who recognize He is the source of strength, the source of success; in Him are health, freedom, abundance, ideas, creativity, and all we need.

Here's the key: if you start getting your daily bread, listening to what God is saying now, and following that still small voice, then you will have your steps for the day and fresh insight into what God wants you to do!

PROMISE:
God has daily favor, daily wisdom, daily ideas, and daily abundance for you. If you'll stay open, He'll lead you into the fullness of your destiny.

Jesus, You are My Bread of Life

Jesus, the Bread of Life, has the power to heal your physical, emotional, and spiritual wounds, offering you abundant life through His sacrifice. He nourishes your soul, satisfies your deepest needs, and empowers you to overcome circumstances that steal your joy and fulfillment. With Jesus, you can live a purposeful, joy-filled, and whole life, knowing He is the source of everything you need for true peace and satisfaction.

DECLARATION PRAYER:
Lord Jesus, You are the Bread of Life, and in You, I find all I need. You satisfy my soul with Your presence, nourish my spirit with Your truth, and sustain me in every season. Whether in times of physical lack, emotional strain, or spiritual challenge, I declare that You are more than enough for me. God, I'm ready. Show me the path, show me how to overcome this challenge, show me how to accomplish my dreams, and give me Your ideas, Your wisdom, and Your direction.

I refuse to allow circumstances to rob me of the abundant, fulfilling life You have given me. I choose to trust in Your provision, for You alone fill my deepest hunger and quench my deepest thirst. In You, I lack nothing. You are my strength and my sustenance.

Jesus, I thank You for the life You purchased for me — a life of purpose, joy, and peace. I will walk in that fullness today, knowing that You are my daily bread, and in You, I will never go hungry.

In Jesus' mighty name, I pray. Amen.

I Am the Door

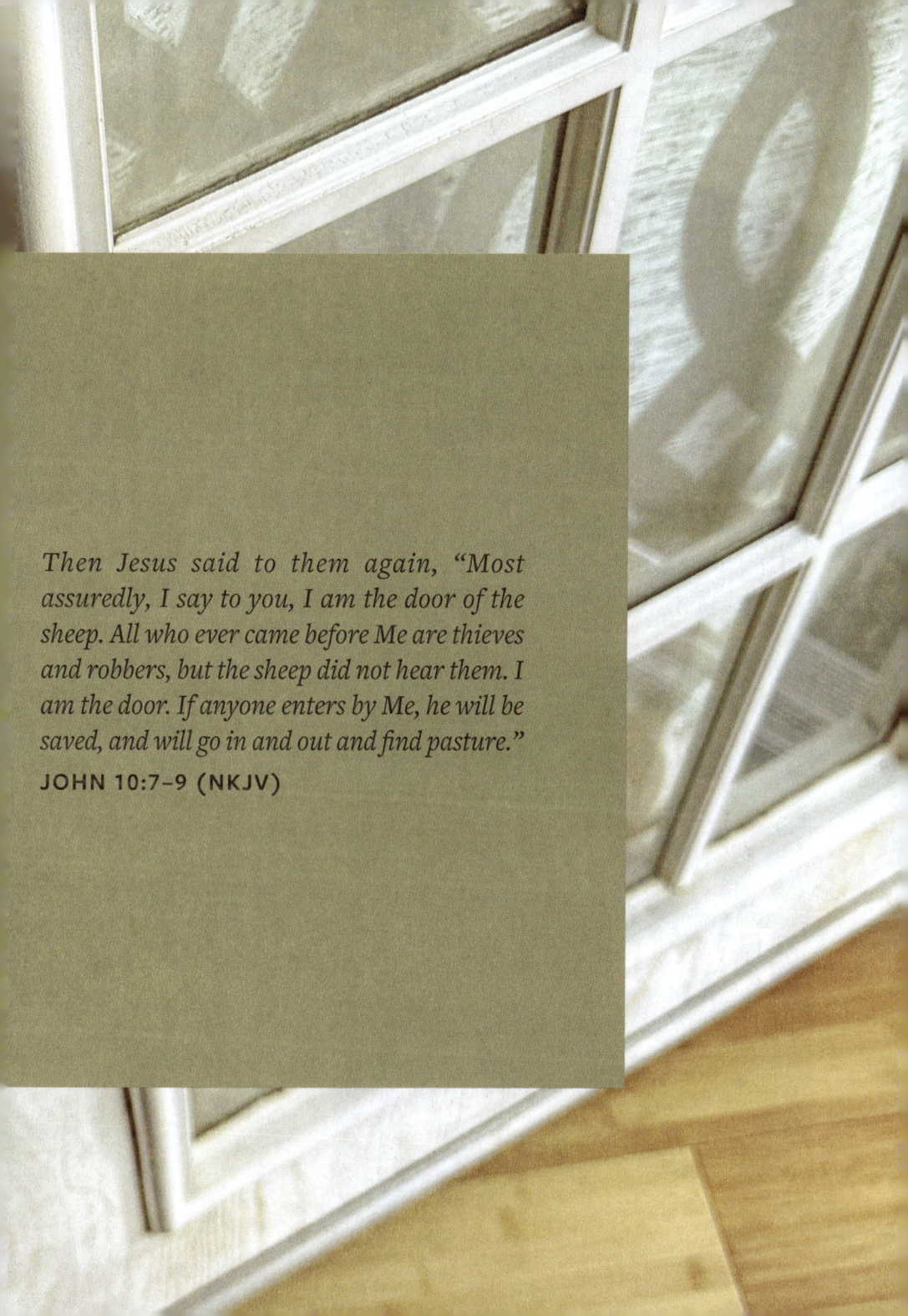

Then Jesus said to them again, "Most assuredly, I say to you, I am the door of the sheep. All who ever came before Me are thieves and robbers, but the sheep did not hear them. I am the door. If anyone enters by Me, he will be saved, and will go in and out and find pasture."

JOHN 10:7–9 (NKJV)

I Am the Door

Jesus is not only the way to your salvation but also the doorway to new opportunities, protection, and the blessings He has promised you.

In John 10:7–9, Jesus uses a metaphor to describe His role as the protector and Savior of those who believe in Him, often called the "sheep."

In ancient times, a shepherd would often lay across the entrance of a sheepfold to protect the flock from harm. When Jesus said, *"I am the door,"* He was likening Himself to this "door" or gate, that He is the way to safety, security, and salvation for His followers.

Jesus said, *"If anyone enters by Me, he will be saved."* Entering through Him — believing in and following Him — leads to eternal life. He is the only true way to salvation.

The Door in the Boat

The earth was filled with corruption and violence, and God decided to cleanse it by washing away humanity. However, one man found favor with God because he was the only one who was righteous. God instructed this devoted and upright father to build a huge boat, a massive vessel, to save himself, his family, and every species of creature on the earth.

That man was Noah, and he obediently followed God's detailed instructions in constructing the boat, which was fully enclosed, to keep Noah, his family, and the animals safe from the coming flood.

When the ark was completed, God commanded Noah, his family, two of every species of creatures, and seven pairs, male and female, of every clean animal, to enter the ark. Then the critical moment came when the Lord shut him in (Genesis 7:16).

God Himself closed the door, sealing Noah and those inside from the dangers outside. The ark's door became the threshold between life and death, safety and destruction, as well as the entrance to new opportunities for Noah and all those in the boat with him.

As the floodwaters rose, the earth drowned, and every creature outside the ark perished. But Noah and his family were safe inside. The closed door protected them from the violent waters, ensuring they would survive for what God had planned for this righteous family. This door became a symbol of both safety and new beginnings, as Noah and those inside were protected from the floodwaters and saved to begin anew.

Shut in by God

"To the angel of the church in Philadelphia write: These are the words of him who is holy and true, who holds the key of David. What He opens no one can shut, and what He shuts no one can open."
REVELATION 3:7 (NIV)

The door, shut by God, was the way He provided salvation and protection. The ark was the only means of survival during the flood. Likewise, Jesus is the "door" to salvation and life for us today, the only way to escape sin and death. We must enter through Him to find refuge and safety. As Noah trusted God's provision and entered the ark, we are called to trust Christ and enter through Him for refuge and eternal life.

Noah's safety wasn't in his efforts but in his obedience to God's provision — the ark. In the same way, our security lies in trusting Christ. It was Noah's strong faith that made him righteous. He obeyed God's command to build the ark and enter it, even when there was no visible sign of the coming flood. We, too, must trust God's word and provision, even when His plan isn't apparent to us.

In His message to the church in Philadelphia, Jesus tells John that He is the only one who can open or shut doors. In other words, Jesus controls access and secures His people by opening or closing opportunities according to His will.

Jesus is the door, the entryway to new possibilities and opportunities. When God opened the door for Noah and his family to come out, they were given a new world, a fresh start, and a new life.

We also must trust God for openings, breakthroughs, and new beginnings He has for us. Even if the promise seems delayed and you feel shut in by uncertainty and discouragement, there will come a day when God opens the door and reveals the new opportunities He's prepared for you.

There will always be people and circumstances that try to keep you behind closed doors. There are forces assigned to you to try to stop your purpose. You may have times when you're behind closed doors, you feel outnumbered, and the odds are against you. You must remind yourself who your Doorkeeper is. Remember, the good news is the forces that are for you are greater than the forces that are against you.

The enemy may have put you behind a door of sickness, trouble, and addiction. You feel shut in, and there's no way out. You must remember what the Word of God says. God will open doors that no

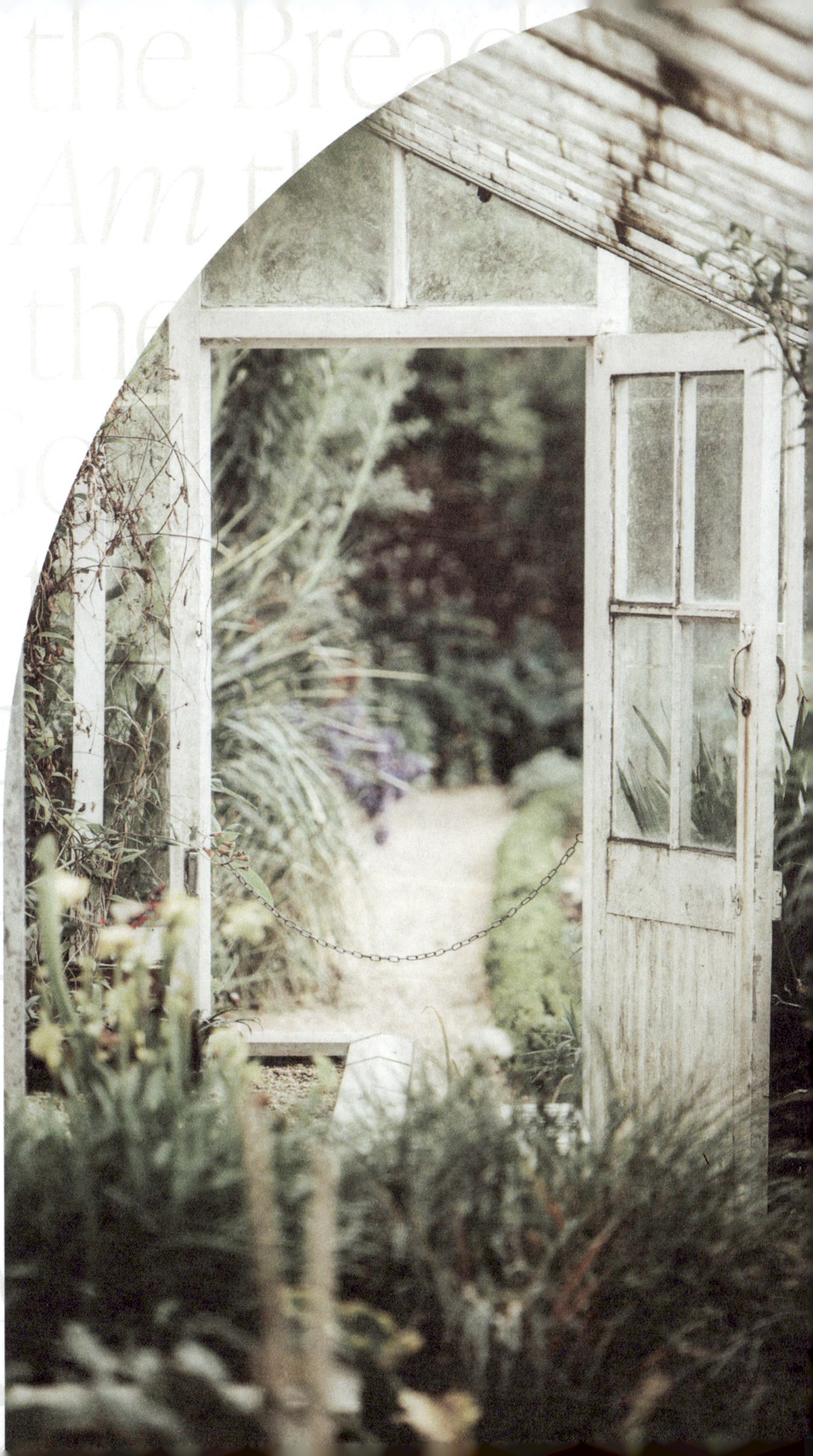

PROMISE: You have the assurance today that what Jesus has opened for you, no one can shut or close your access to it.

person can shut. Your time is coming. God won't let you get into a problem He can't get you out of. He wouldn't have let that door close if He didn't have a way to open it.

Good Pastures

> "I tell you the truth, I am the gate for the sheep. All who came before me were thieves and robbers. But the true sheep did not listen to them. Yes, I am the gate. Those who come in through me will be saved. They will come and go freely and will find good pastures."
> **JOHN 10:7–9 (NLT)**

There is a promise here on not just "pastures" for the Good Shepherd's sheep but "good pastures." There is abundant goodness, spiritual nourishment, perfect peace, and total freedom that Jesus offers those who follow Him. In Him, believers will find complete fulfillment and maximum security.

Perhaps doors that have been closed in your family for generations are about to open. Addictions, depression, low self-esteem, and mediocrity — those old barriers are being unlocked. Like Noah, you're about to enter the new world God has prepared for you, walking into blessings, freedom, wholeness, success, and new levels.

Maybe your family has had a history of depression, sickness, heart disease, divorce, or division. It may feel like you've been shut out, but the door is about to open. God is releasing you into increase, new levels, and blessings you've never seen. It's not because of anything you've done — it's the Doorkeeper, showing you favor, bringing the right people into your life, freeing you from addiction, and lifting you out of struggle and lack into abundance.

I see chains breaking, locks falling off, and doors opening. You're coming out of generational curses, limitations, and struggles, stepping into generational blessings. What has been stored up for your family is about to be released through you. What's been held back, what should have been yours — it's not lost; it's been accumulating. This isn't something you could make happen — it's the King of Glory, your door, doing what only He can do. So, get ready for open doors!

Jesus said He is the door to good pastures — a good life, living, and opportunities. Let this truth settle in your spirit: doors are about to open. God will take you where you could never go on your own. The chains that have kept those doors deadbolted and locked may seem permanent, but they are no match for the Most High God.

PROMISE:
Today, you are assured that Jesus will bring you into "good pastures" — abundant goodness, spiritual nourishment, and total freedom — where you will find complete fulfillment and perfect safety.

Joel Osteen

Abundant Living

Every good and perfect gift is from above, coming down from the Father of the heavenly lights, with whom there is no change or shifting shadow.
JAMES 1:17 (BSB)

Jesus, our door, grants us access to abundant life. Just as a door allows entry into a place of security and provision, Jesus is the gateway to the fullness of life God intends for us. Through Him, we find good pastures, nourishment, and spiritual guidance to thrive.

Jesus is your access to freedom, healing, provision, and blessing. Walk through the door and draw close to the Great Shepherd. Everything you need is found in Him. King David wrote, *"The Lord is my shepherd; I shall not want"* (Psalm 23:1, NKJV).

Jesus declares that He is the only door for the sheep. He is the rock in the wilderness, providing living water. He is the Great High Priest, interceding before the Father on our behalf. He is the veil torn in the temple, granting us access to the Father's presence. He is the atoning sacrifice, paying for our salvation. He is the Great Shepherd who brings safety and provision to His people. Jesus is the only way the sheep enter the fold and go out to find good pasture.

Today, we can walk through the door Jesus has opened for us. He gave His life so we could enter into healing, freedom, promotion, and fulfillment of His promises. I believe and declare that Jesus, the door, is opening opportunities in your business, breakthroughs in your health, restoration in your relationships, and an increase in your finances. Like Noah, doors are about to open to a new world of freedom, healing, divine connections, and new levels of destiny in Jesus' name.

Opportunity and good things await you. Walk through the gate and enter into a place of secure protection and abundant provision, in Jesus' name.

Jesus, You are My Door

Jesus is my door to new opportunities. Jesus has shut doors to protect me from harm and opened doors to find good pastures.

DECLARATION PRAYER:

Heavenly Father, I come before You, declaring Your greatness and majesty over all creation. You are the door, the gatekeeper, the refuge, and the strong fortress in whom I place my trust. Lord Jesus, You are my door — through You, I enter into the abundant life of Your Kingdom.

I declare that You are my source of comfort and rest, just as You were for Noah, delivering him and his family from destruction. You are my shield and protector, the One who opens doors that no one can shut and shuts doors that no one can open. I am secure in Your presence when you shut the door.

Father, I declare that in every season, You alone are the key to my security and provision. Through You, I have access to the fullness of life and the nearness of the Father. You have always been the source of comfort, peace, and salvation, and You continue to lead me on paths of righteousness for Your name's sake.

Your promises are my refuge, and I stand firm, knowing that You are the gate through which I enter into Your presence, where there is fullness of joy and abundant living.

I praise You, Lord, for You are my redeemer and the door to all the good things you have for me.

In Jesus' name. Amen.

I Am the Light

Jesus spoke to the people once more and said, "I am the light of the world. If you follow me, you won't have to walk in darkness, because you will have the light that leads to life."

JOHN 8:12 (NLT)

I Am the Light

Jesus lights your path, providing protection and direction in your life.

Jesus is the source of **truth and guidance in a dark world**. His light reveals what is hidden and **guides us every step of the way**, ensuring that we are never left alone. By following His light, we are led to life, and His presence provides **direction and clarity** in all circumstances.

Even in times of darkness, Jesus is at work, bringing new things into our lives. Instead of being discouraged, we can thank Him through difficult seasons, knowing that darkness will always give way to the light of His plans. No force of darkness can stop what God has ordained for you.

A Flashing Light

There was a man named Saul, a devout Pharisee and a passionate persecutor of Christians determined to stamp out the early Christian movement known as "the Way." Saul obtained letters from the high priest, giving him the authority to arrest any Christians he found in Damascus and bring them back to Jerusalem for punishment. Saul set out on the road to Damascus with these letters, eager to accomplish his mission.

As he neared Damascus, a bright light from Heaven suddenly flashed around him. The light was so intense that it blinded Saul, and he fell to the ground.

He heard a voice saying, *"Saul, Saul, why do you persecute Me?"* (Acts 9:4, NIV)

Confused and frightened, Saul asked, *"Who are you, Lord?"* (v. 5).

The voice replied, *"I am Jesus, whom you are persecuting . . . Now get up and go into the city, and you will be told what you must do"* (vv. 5–6).

Saul's encounter with the Light of the World radically changed his life. He went from being a fierce persecutor of Christians to becoming one of Jesus' most passionate and influential apostles. When the light shined into the darkness of Saul's heart, he was profoundly transformed.

Saul's experience reveals how encountering the Light of the World can completely change a person's direction in life. Saul's conversion began his new mission to spread the message of Christ to the gentiles. He would write many of the letters that make up the New Testament that have given illumination to God's people for two thousand years.

That one encounter with Jesus changed Saul's name, upended his life, and impacted the course of Christian history. He became Paul, one of the most influential apostles in the early Christian church. Through his missionary work, theological writings, and dedication to the Gospel, Paul played a crucial role in spreading Christianity throughout the Roman Empire and making Christianity a global faith.

A Great Light

The people who walk in darkness will see a great light. For those who live in a land of deep darkness, a light will shine.
ISAIAH 9:2 (NLT)

When Jesus said, *"I am the light of the world"* (John 8:12, NIV), He was in the Second Temple in Jerusalem. The sun was rising in the east, the direction in which the Messiah would come, and the religious leaders knew He was declaring Himself to be the Anointed One (Isaiah 9:2).

PROMISE:
No matter your past, His light has the power to illuminate your path and lead you into a life of meaning and impact.

PROMISE:
When you believe in and follow Jesus, the Light of the World, you will no longer live in darkness but receive the light of life, leading to a life of abundance, free from doubt and fear.

When Jesus pointed to the extinguished lamps representing God's presence and declared, *"I am the light of the world,"* He indicated He was God's true and living presence. We don't have to live in the darkness of doubt and fear. Instead, we receive the light of life, believe in Him, and follow Him, which leads us to an abundant life.

The Glory of the Lord

"Arise, shine, for your light has come, and the glory of the Lord rises upon you."
ISAIAH 60:1 (NIV)

Esther was an orphan with no parents to guide her, seemingly powerless in her situation. Yet her uncle entered her into a beauty contest, and the prize was meeting the king. Against all odds, she won and became queen. When the Jews faced annihilation due to the king's decree (Esther 3), Esther did the unthinkable — she entered the king's chamber unannounced, risking not only her position but her life.

Her attitude was one of bold faith: "I've been raised up for such a time as this." She didn't shrink back in fear, thinking of the "what ifs" — what if he gets upset, what if he says no, what if my family is affected? Instead, she took the risk, knowing that for a mighty exploit to happen, faith was required. Where there are no risks, there are no awe-inspiring deeds.

God has some things only He can do, and the way to activate that faith is by stepping out, by arising. Know that you are glorious, a mighty warrior, and that the Most High God is backing you up. He has said, "I myself have blessed you." So, arise and shine, for the glory of God is upon you.

You are called to go out and perform awe-inspiring deeds, but remember, you must first arise. You can't sit back and wait for things to happen; you must activate your faith. As Isaiah 60:2 says, *"Darkness covers the earth and thick darkness is over the peoples, but the* Lord *rises upon you and his glory appears over you"* (NIV).

Throughout Israel's history, God manifested His glory as a glowing cloud or pillar of fire in the Old Testament. This glory of the Lord appeared as radiant, flaming fire within the cloud, providing light and guidance for the Israelites.

The cloud hovered over the tabernacle, filled the temple when it was built, and appeared between the cherubim above the mercy seat, behind the veil in the holy of holies. When Jesus declared, *"I am the light of the world"* (John 9:5, NIV), He revealed He was that light.

Jesus is the source of truth and guidance in a dark world. In Scripture, light symbolizes belief, while darkness represents unbelief (John 1:9–13). Jesus is described as *"The true light that gives light to everyone"*

PROMISE: Jesus, your light has come, and **His glory** is shining on you and through you. He can guide you through every trial and obstacle you face.

PROMISE: Darkness must always give way to Jesus, the light, which leads to life. In Him, you find your promise, your path, and your victory.

(John 1:9, NIV). His light is more powerful than the temple lights, the radiant clouds, or even the sun. Jesus is both the possessor and the giver of light, illuminating the path to life for all who follow Him.

Can't Stop the Light

> *In Him was life, and that life was **the light of all mankind**. The light shines in the darkness, and the darkness has not overcome it.*
> **JOHN 1:4–5 (NIV)**

Before light appears, there is darkness. In the beginning, darkness covered the deep, and God said, *"Let there be light"* (Genesis 1:3, NIV). The light drove away the darkness. Darkness means light is coming. Change is about to happen. The promise is about to come. Who can stop the sun from rising each morning? Who can keep the light from breaking over the horizon?

All the darkness in Saul's heart couldn't stop the Light of the World from suddenly coming. Likewise, all the forces of darkness cannot stop what God has ordained for you. They cannot keep what He promised from coming to pass.

Thank Him in the Dark

*The LORD **is my light** and my salvation; whom shall I fear? The LORD is the stronghold of my life; of whom shall I be afraid?*
PSALM 27:1 (ESV)

And God called the firmament Heaven. So the evening and the morning were the second day.
GENESIS 1:8 (NKJV)

In God's Kingdom, He begins His work in darkness and moves toward light. Each day of creation starts with evening (darkness) and ends with morning (light), showing that God brings new things into existence out of chaos and darkness. His creative process is intentional, turning what is hidden or unseen into something filled with purpose and life.

God often works in the hidden or dark moments of our lives to bring transformation and new beginnings. Just as physical light follows the evening, spiritual light follows seasons of difficulty and uncertainty. God's creative power moves us from darkness into light, from confusion into clarity, and from brokenness into wholeness.

In the face of darkness, when you don't yet see any light, declare, "Father, thank You. It's a new day. It may still be dark, but I trust what I know: My healing is coming, my breakthrough is coming, my victory is coming because You, Jesus, are my light."

PROMISE:
You can have confidence that God is already working in the darkness of night, preparing your new day as the light begins to dawn.

When you understand that Jesus often starts with darkness to bring about new things, you won't be discouraged by it. Instead, you'll thank Him during it and praise Him despite any obstacles.

Getting Direction

Your word is a lamp to my feet and a light to my path.
PSALM 119:105 (ESV)

Believing and trusting in Jesus brings into our lives light and life. We are guided by His light, walking not in darkness but in the light of life. His light reveals what is hidden and directs every step. Reading God's Word gives us wisdom and guidance throughout life.

Just as a lamp lights our way in the dark, God's Word provides clarity and direction when we face life's challenges. When Scripture speaks of a lamp to guide our feet, that is God's guidance, revealing each step, moment by moment. But it doesn't end there — He also promises to be a light to our paths, showing us how to live in accordance with His will, lighting the way forward not only in immediate decisions but for the broader journey.

We are never left alone as Jesus lights our way. Our role is to follow Him and obey Him by responding to His direction. We must follow it and walk in it, our path — our way of life.

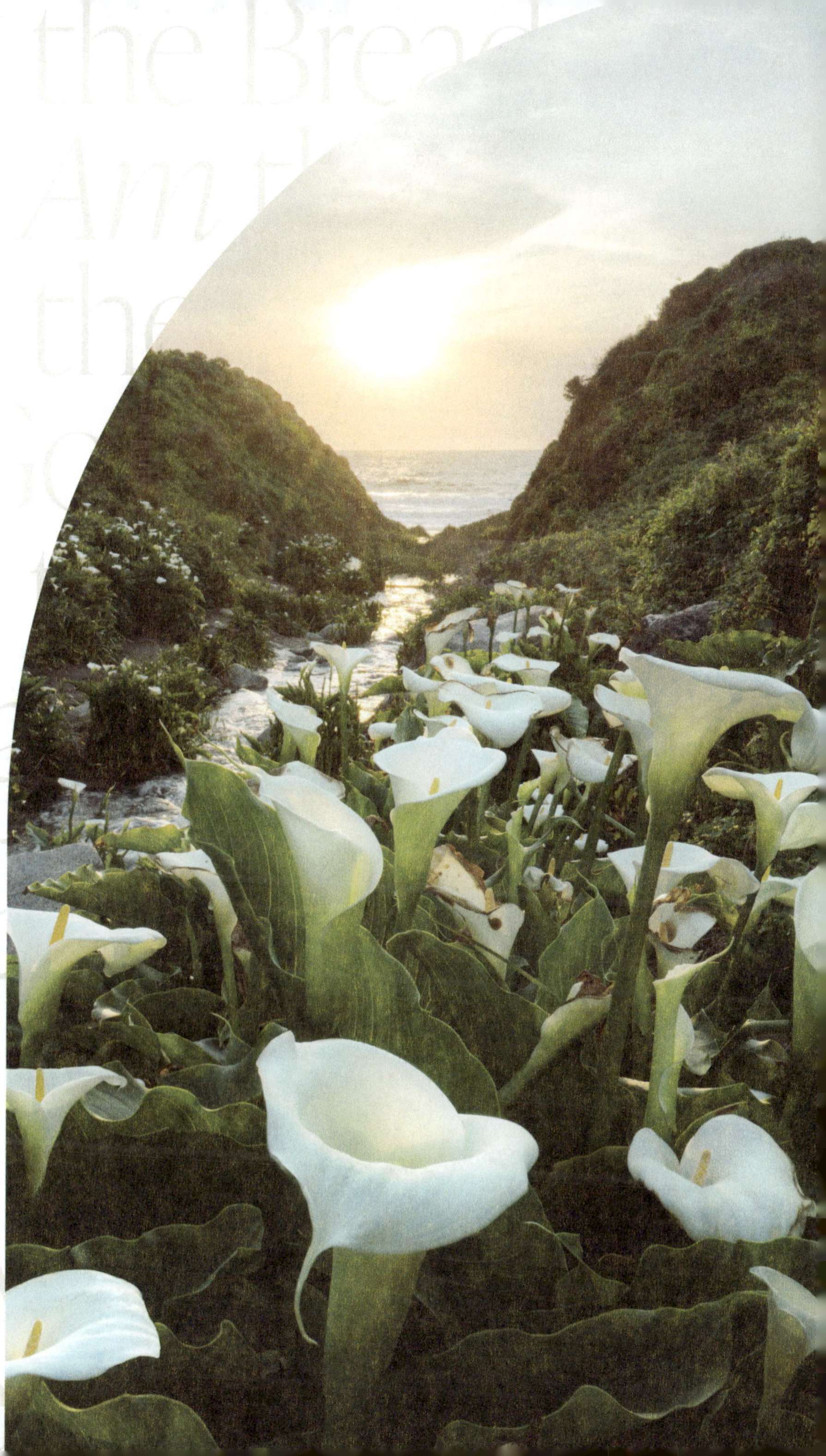

Jesus, You are My Light

Jesus, the Light of the World, illuminates your path, offering you protection and guidance in every step of life. When you place your trust in Him and follow His lead, darkness no longer has power over you. You will walk in the light that brings life — abundant, fearless, and full of promise.

His glory shines on you and through you, guiding you through every challenge and obstacle. No matter how dark the night, Jesus' light will always break through, leading you to victory, purpose, and the fulfillment of His promises. Trust that even in the darkest moments, God is working, preparing a bright new day for you.

DECLARATION PRAYER:

Heavenly Father, I come before You in awe and gratitude for sending Jesus, the Light of the World, into my life. Jesus, You declared that You are the light, and in You, I find clarity, protection, and direction. I thank You for not having to walk in darkness because Your light leads me to life.

Just as the light shone upon Saul on the road to Damascus and transformed him into Paul, I thank You that Your light shines into my heart, bringing transformation, revelation, and purpose. All the darkness within me and around me cannot stop the light You have placed in my life. Your light dispels the shadows of doubt, fear, and unbelief.

I declare that Your glory rises upon me. No force of darkness can extinguish what You have ordained for me. As I face challenges, I will thank You in the darkness, knowing that Your light will break through. I walk by faith, not by what I see, knowing that the breakthrough, healing, and victory are already mine.

I stand firm in the promise that Your light reveals the way forward, guiding my every step. I submit to Your will and follow You, for You are the true light that gives life to all mankind. As I walk in Your light, I declare that it will shine through me, touching those around me and drawing them to Your truth.

Jesus, my light, my hope, my guide — thank You for leading me out of darkness and into the fullness of life.

In Jesus' name. Amen.

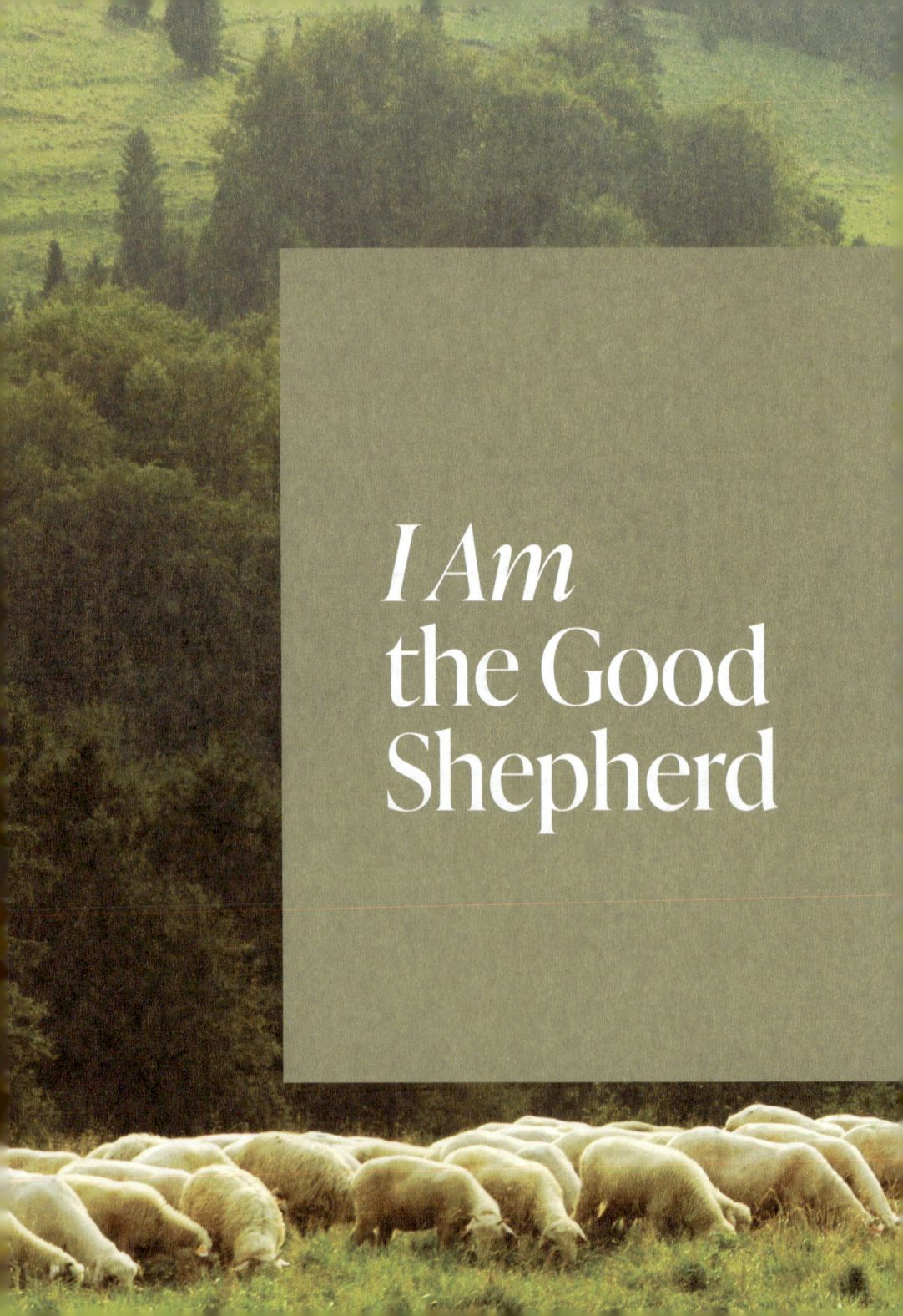

I Am the Good Shepherd

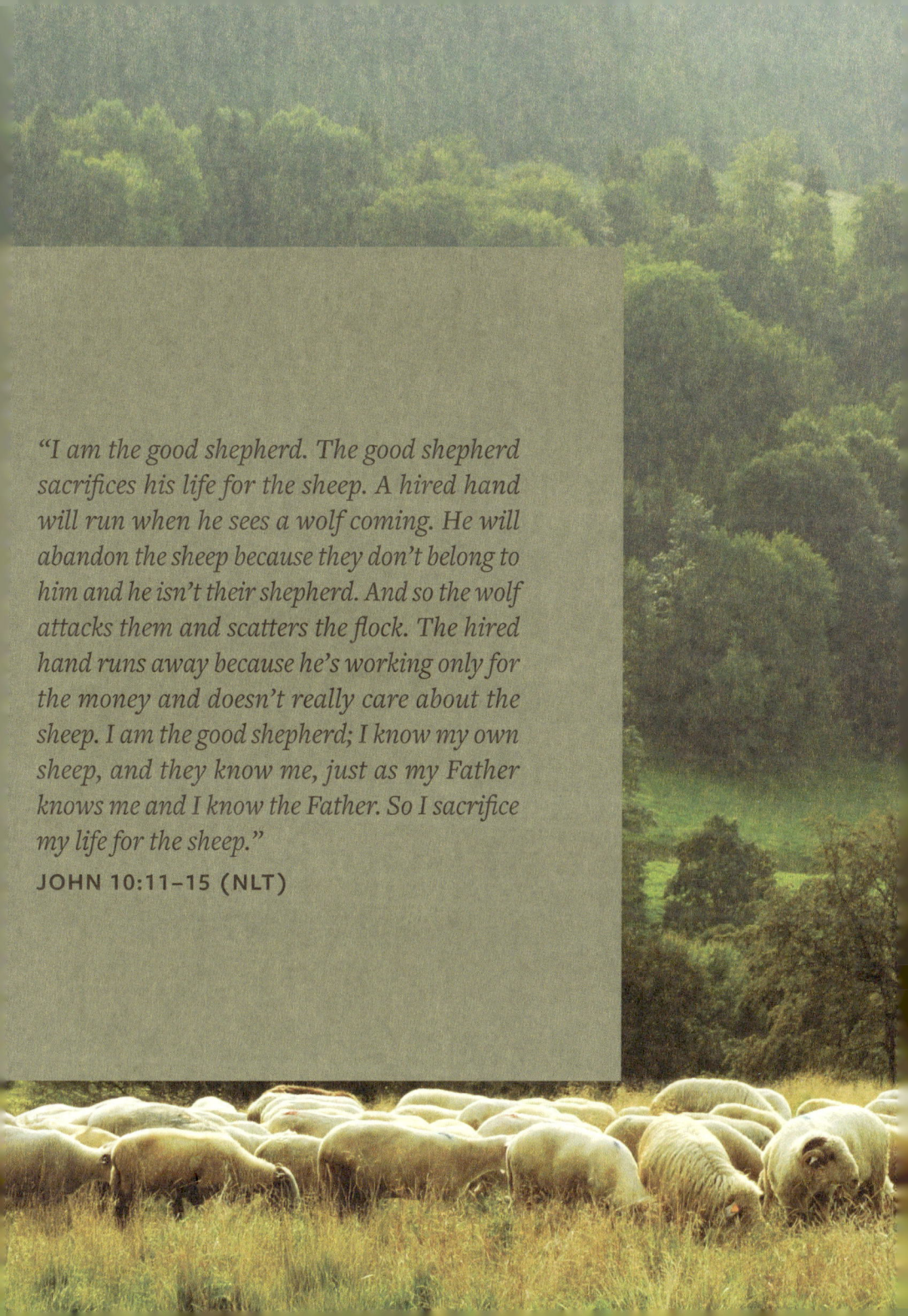

"I am the good shepherd. The good shepherd sacrifices his life for the sheep. A hired hand will run when he sees a wolf coming. He will abandon the sheep because they don't belong to him and he isn't their shepherd. And so the wolf attacks them and scatters the flock. The hired hand runs away because he's working only for the money and doesn't really care about the sheep. I am the good shepherd; I know my own sheep, and they know me, just as my Father knows me and I know the Father. So I sacrifice my life for the sheep."

JOHN 10:11–15 (NLT)

I Am the Good Shepherd

Jesus declares He is the One who cares for and protects His followers like a shepherd does with his sheep.

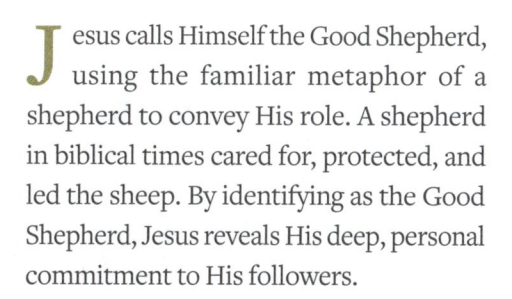

Jesus calls Himself the Good Shepherd, using the familiar metaphor of a shepherd to convey His role. A shepherd in biblical times cared for, protected, and led the sheep. By identifying as the Good Shepherd, Jesus reveals His deep, personal commitment to His followers.

The word good here not only refers to moral goodness but also conveys the ideas of nobility, worthiness, and selflessness. Jesus is the ideal shepherd who embodies perfect care and love.

When Jesus says the Good Shepherd sacrifices his life for the sheep, He reveals the depth of His protective nature.

A good shepherd would risk his life to defend his flock, but Jesus takes this further, declaring that He willingly lays down His life for His people. This foreshadows His ultimate sacrifice on the cross for humanity's salvation. Unlike hired workers who might flee in danger, the Good Shepherd stays faithful, even to the point of death, showing the depth of His love and commitment to those who follow Him.

PROMISE:
Your prayers and faith invite His mercy, and His grace extends beyond what is deserved, offering protection and second chances.

Young Man Falls to Near Death

I heard about a young man, just twenty-one years old, who had grown up in church. He knew what was right, but he drifted away, getting involved in partying, drinking, and running with the wrong crowd. Through it all, his mother was back home praying faithfully for him, constantly reaching out to encourage him to turn his life around — but he wouldn't listen.

One night, after drinking far too much, some of his friends dared him to climb a power pole. In his reckless state, he agreed. He made it about forty feet up, climbing while heavily intoxicated. As he neared the top, he lost his footing and fell.

At that moment, as he was plummeting toward what seemed like a certain death, his leather belt somehow snagged on a metal rod protruding from the pole, acting like a harness and stopping his fall. He dangled there in the dead of night until rescuers arrived and brought him down safely.

The next day, the newspaper headline read, "Pants Save Drunk Man from Fall." But that was more than a headline — it was God's mercy, His protection in action.

Parents, those prayers you've been praying for your children — they make a difference. Even if they act foolishly and recklessly, they may not deserve God's protection. But because of your prayers, faith, and steadfastness, Jesus, our Great Shepherd, can and will protect them, even when they don't deserve it.

Asleep in the Storm

Jesus was sleeping at the back of the boat with his head on a cushion. The disciples woke him up, shouting, "Teacher, don't you care that we're going to drown?"
MARK 4:38 (NLT)

After a day of teaching by the Sea of Galilee, Jesus tells His disciples, *"Let us go over to the other side"* (Mark 4:35, NIV). Leaving the crowd behind, they set out in a boat with Jesus. As they cross the sea, a fierce storm suddenly arises, and waves crash over the boat, threatening to swamp it.

Despite the violent storm, Jesus is in the stern, peacefully sleeping. The disciples, terrified by the storm and fearing for their lives, wake Him and say, *"Teacher, don't you care if we drown?"* (v. 38).

Jesus gets up and says to the wind and the waves, *"Quiet! Be still!"* (v. 39). Immediately, the wind dies down, and there is complete calm. Jesus then turns to His disciples and asks, *"Why are you so afraid? Do you still have no faith?"* (v. 40).

The disciples were amazed and said to each other, *"Who is this? Even the wind and the waves obey him!"*

PROMISE: Jesus cares for you and is your protector even in the midst of your storms.

(v. 41). This event leaves them marveling at Jesus' authority over the natural world.

Why Are You Afraid?

"Why are you so afraid? Do you still have no faith?"
MARK 4:40 (NIV)

It deepens our faith, knowing that Jesus, who has power over all creation, including the winds and the waves, is our protector and deliverer. Calming the storm and gently rebuking the disciples shows that He cares deeply for their well-being and our state of mind. He brings peace amid chaos and protects and cares for those who follow Him.

Jesus' question, "Why are you so afraid?" challenges us to trust Him, even when circumstances seem dire. It underscores the importance of faith in Jesus' power and presence, especially when facing life's storms.

The disciples' fear shifts from focus on the storm to a reverential awe of Jesus. This shift in focus — from the threat to the One who controls it — teaches us to trust in Jesus' power to protect and deliver us, no matter how frightening our circumstances might be.

PROMISE:
Trust in Jesus' presence and power, and He will protect and deliver you, no matter the storms or circumstances you face.

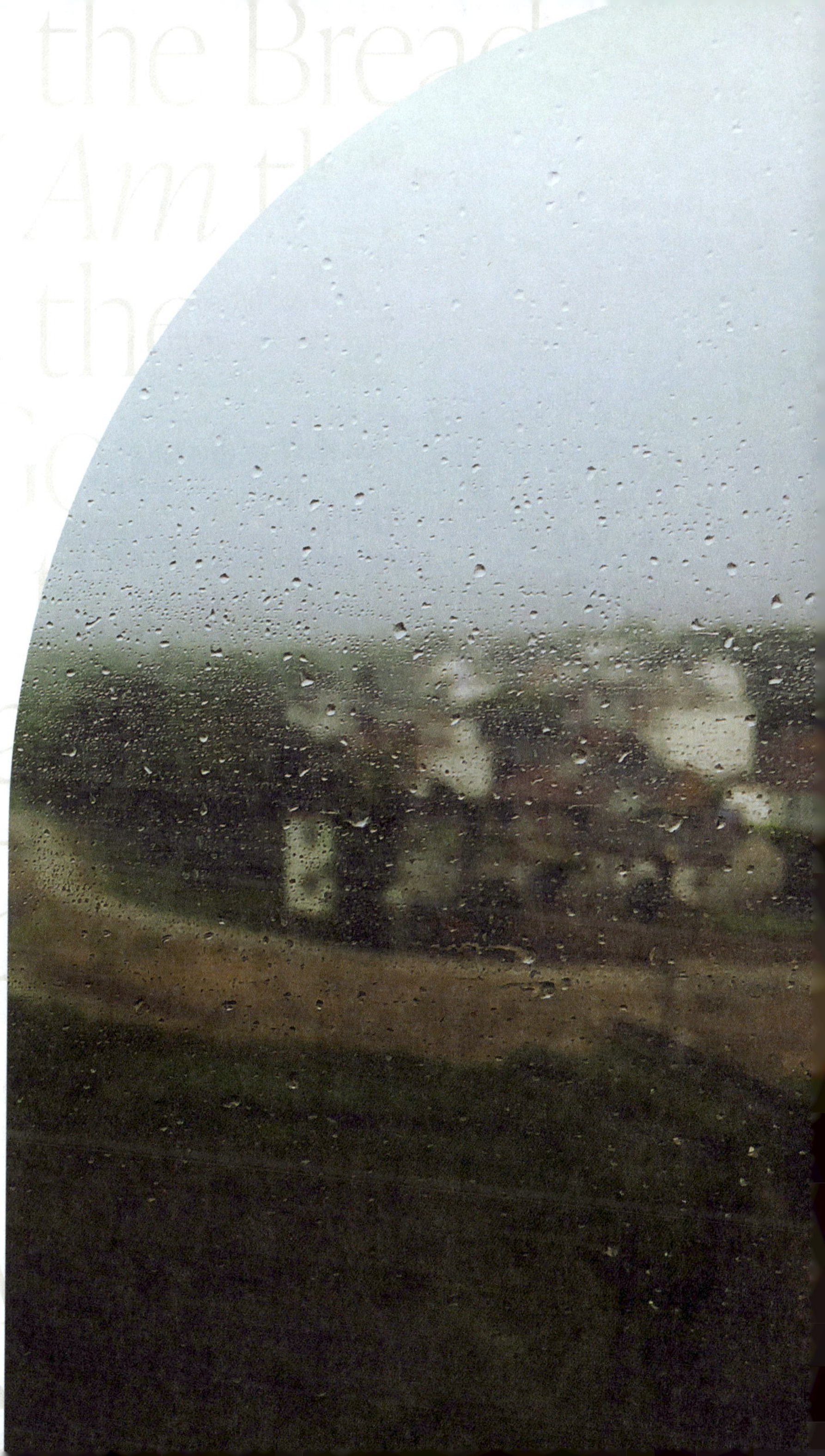

False Shepherds

> *"A hired hand will run when he sees a wolf coming. He will abandon the sheep because they don't belong to him and he isn't their shepherd. And so the wolf attacks them and scatters the flock. The hired hand runs away because he's working only for the money and doesn't really care about the sheep."*
> **JOHN 10:12–13 (NLT)**

Jesus said, "All who ever came before Me are thieves and robbers, but the sheep did not hear them" (John 10:8, NKJV), referring to false messiahs, leaders, or religious figures who misled people. Jesus is teaching His followers (the sheep) not to listen to these false leaders.

Jesus warns us of false shepherds (or hirelings) who abandon the sheep when danger comes. These false leaders do not genuinely care for the flock. Jesus, on the other hand, is the true shepherd who is entirely devoted to His sheep, the only One who can be our savior and protector.

This passage contrasts the **hired hand** with Jesus, the **Good Shepherd**. The hired hand symbolizes leaders or people who are motivated by self-interest rather than genuine care for others. When danger approaches, such as a wolf, the hired hand runs away to protect himself, leaving the sheep vulnerable to attack.

This lack of care is because the sheep don't belong to him, and he has no real sense of responsibility or connection to them. His primary concern is his own safety and financial gain, not the flock's well-being.

In contrast, Jesus, the true shepherd, sincerely cares for His people and is willing to sacrifice everything, even His life, to protect and guide them. It also serves as a warning against following false leaders who care more about personal gain than the spiritual well-being of others, encouraging believers to trust in Jesus, the Good Shepherd, who will never abandon them.

PROMISE: Jesus, the true shepherd, knows and cares for you.

The Shepherd Watches

GOD's your Guardian, right at your side to protect you — shielding you from sunstroke, sheltering you from moonstroke. GOD guards you from every evil, he guards your very life. He guards you when you leave and when you return, He guards you now, he guards you always.
PSALM 121:5–7 (MSG)

The Lord is your protector — your shield, your strong tower, your defender, and your fortress. Whom shall you fear?

God watched over His people, Israel, as they journeyed through the desert, steadily advancing toward their promised destiny. Scripture tells us:

PROMISE:
You can be assured that, as your Shepherd, God is always watching over you, guarding you from harm in every area of your life.

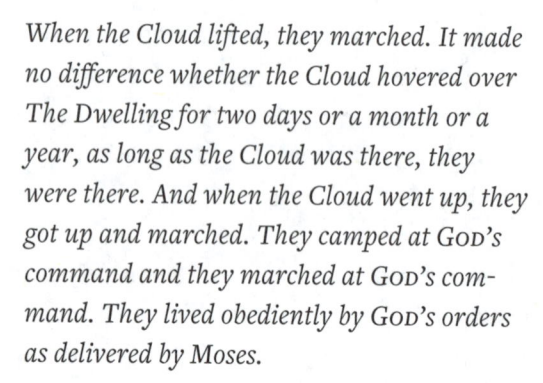

When the Cloud lifted, they marched. It made no difference whether the Cloud hovered over The Dwelling for two days or a month or a year, as long as the Cloud was there, they were there. And when the Cloud went up, they got up and marched. They camped at GOD's command and they marched at GOD's command. They lived obediently by GOD's orders as delivered by Moses.

NUMBERS 9:21–23 (MSG)

Bishop T.D. Jakes shared a powerful testimony of what happened to him. One Sunday morning, just as he was about to get dressed for church, a massive explosion shook his house. The entire back end was blown apart. In his basement, a group of large heaters had built up pressure due to poor ventilation, causing the explosion.

Typically, at that time of morning, he would have been in that part of the house getting ready. But just a few weeks earlier, he had decided to move his Sunday morning service from 8:00 a.m. to 9:00 a.m. If he hadn't made that change, he would have been in those rooms when the explosion occurred — and he might not be with us today.

Friends, you have a protector. The Most High God is watching over you. You're not going through life alone, hoping things will work out. The Creator of the universe has placed a hedge of protection around you that cannot be penetrated without His permission.

This means that as long as you dwell in the secret place of His presence, nothing can happen to you by accident. That's not to say you'll never face challenges or accidents, but it does mean that none of it will surprise God.

Just as a shepherd watches over his sheep, God watches over His people. And just like those sheep, we must faithfully follow Him. When the Shepherd moves, we move; when the Shepherd stops, we stop. Though we are surrounded by danger and uncertainty, our safety lies in staying close to the Good Shepherd and obediently resting in His presence.

It's About Relationship

"I am the good shepherd; I know my own sheep, and my sheep know me, just as my Father knows me and I know the Father. So I sacrifice my life for the sheep. I have other sheep, too, that are not in this sheepfold. I must bring them also. They will listen to my voice, and there will be one flock with one shepherd."
JOHN 10:14–16 (NLT)

When Jesus says, "I am the good shepherd," He shares something abundantly meaningful with those who follow Him. Shepherding was a familiar occupation to those He was speaking to. God often used the image of a shepherd caring for his sheep to describe His relationship with His people.

PROMISE:
As your Good Shepherd, Jesus knows you personally and intimately.

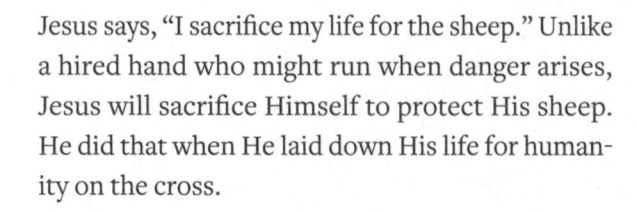

Jesus says, "I sacrifice my life for the sheep." Unlike a hired hand who might run when danger arises, Jesus will sacrifice Himself to protect His sheep. He did that when He laid down His life for humanity on the cross.

He is describing the intimate and personal relationship He desires with His followers. He knows each one by name and cares for them individually. They know His voice, and He knows them. This mutual trust reflects the deep bond between the shepherd and his sheep. This is the power and nature of faith in Jesus.

The image of the shepherd also connects to Old Testament passages where God declares Himself the Shepherd of Israel (Psalm 23; Psalm 80:1; Isaiah 40:11; Ezekiel 34:11–16). By calling Himself the Good Shepherd, Jesus identifies Himself with these divine promises, revealing He is the Messiah who has come to fulfill God's covenant and care for His people.

The Shepherd Provides

The LORD is my shepherd; I shall not want.
PSALM 23:1 (NKJV)

David is using the image of a shepherd to show us God's care and provision. A shepherd was responsible for guiding, protecting, and providing for their sheep, completely dependent on the shepherd for food, water, safety, and direction. Just as a shepherd is always present to care for the sheep, God is intimately involved in every aspect of David's life.

David knows that under God's care, he will never be in need. He trusts that God will provide everything necessary for his physical, emotional, and spiritual well-being. David finds peace in knowing God is always with him, ensuring he has everything he needs. David completely trusted God's guidance, protection, and loving provision. He knew God as his shepherd and had complete faith in Him.

Jesus' ultimate act of provision is His sacrifice on the cross. He gave His life to redeem us from sin and reconcile us to God. As John 10:11 states, *"I am the good shepherd. The good shepherd lays down his life for the sheep"* (NIV). This sacrificial love is the cornerstone of our salvation.

PROMISE:
He is your Good Shepherd. He will provide for all your needs, and because of Him, you will lack nothing. He offers guidance, protection, and care in every situation.

Jesus, You are My Shepherd

For believers, the presence of Jesus, our Good Shepherd, is a source of comfort and assurance, providing constant care, protection, guidance, and the ultimate sacrifice for our salvation.

Jesus revealed Himself as Israel's shepherd so we, as believers, would trust His leadership, follow His voice, and rest in the security that He provides as our Good Shepherd. In Him, we lack nothing.

DECLARATION PRAYER:

Heavenly Father, You are my Good Shepherd, and I am Your sheep. I declare that You know me intimately, and I know Your voice. You laid down Your life for me, demonstrating the depth of Your love and care. You are my protector, my provider, and my deliverer. In You, I lack nothing.

As I follow You, I trust in Your leadership and guidance. Just as the shepherd moves and the sheep follow, I will follow You, knowing that You lead me into paths of righteousness and peace. Even in the face of danger or uncertainty, I will not fear, for Your presence surrounds me.

You watch over me, guiding me through every storm and difficulty. I declare that no harm can touch me without Your permission, for You have placed a hedge of protection around my life. When chaos arises, You speak peace. When I am weary, You restore my soul.

Thank You, Jesus, for Your unfailing love, for knowing my needs before I even ask, and for being the shepherd who never leaves His flock. I trust in You completely, for You are my refuge and strength, my ever-present help.

In Jesus' name. Amen.

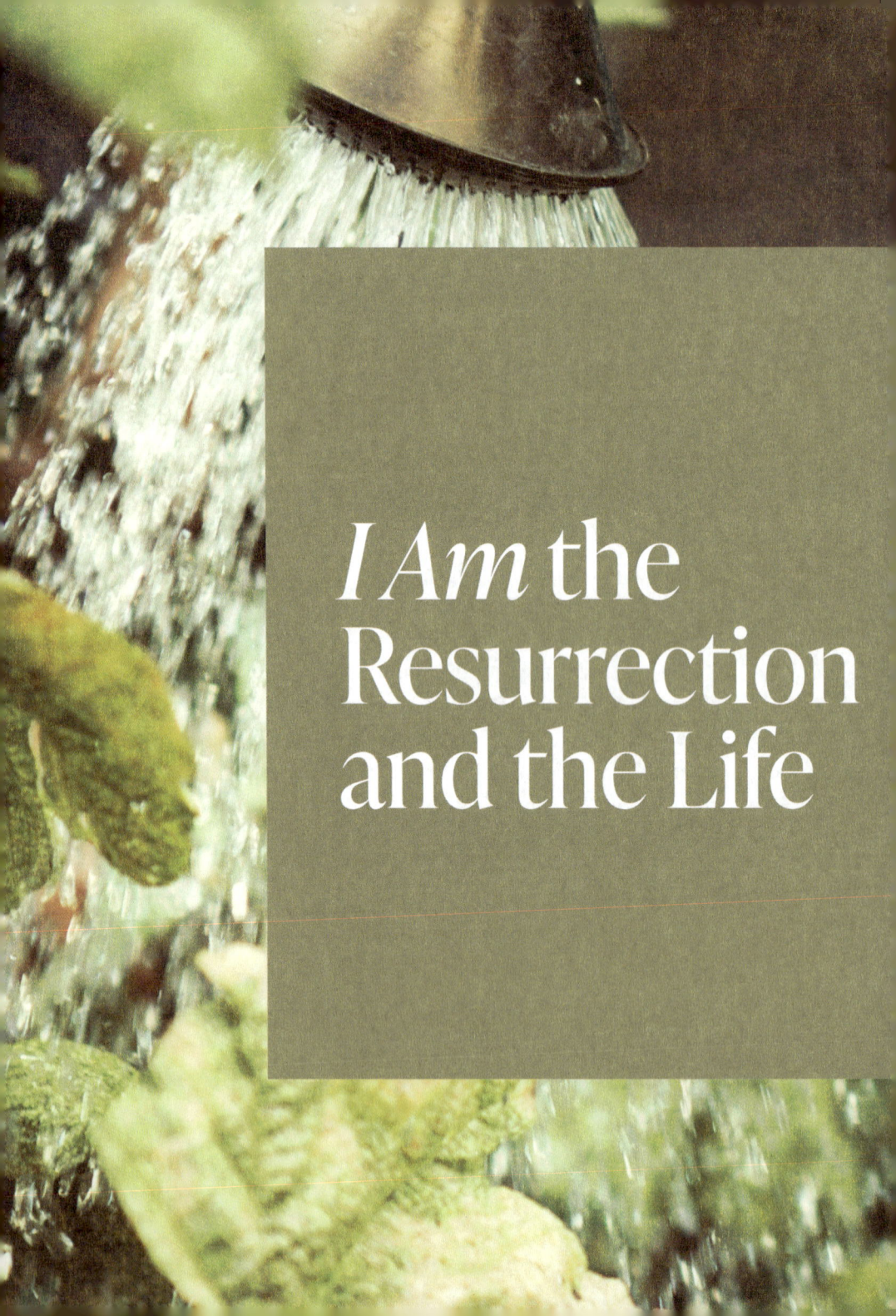

I Am the Resurrection and the Life

"I am the resurrection and the life. The one who believes in me will live, even though they die; and whoever lives by believing in me will never die. Do you believe this?"

JOHN 11:25–26 (NIV)

I Am the Resurrection and the Life

Jesus gives you power over anything in your life that needs to be resurrected or restored. He holds power over life and death, both physically and spiritually. For believers, this means that through faith in Him, they have the promise of resurrection after death and the gift of eternal life in the presence of God. Jesus alone is the way to eternal life, giving us hope and victory over death.

When Jesus says, "I Am," He connects Himself to the Father — the Great I Am. By saying, *"I am the resurrection and the life,"* He reveals the authority and power given to Him over life and death.

Jesus is the source of resurrection life and rebirth. He holds all available power and gives eternal life to everyone who believes. The spiritual life He offers is not only for the future but is available to us now, transforming our lives in this life and after death.

Dead Man Walks

Jesus loved Mary, Martha, and Lazarus and often spent much time with them. They were very close and had deep affection for each other. One day, Lazarus, whose name means "God my help," came down with a terrible sickness and was burning up with fever. Mary and Martha sent word to Jesus, who was on the other side of the Jordan River from Bethany, to come quickly.

But when Jesus heard about it, he said, "Lazarus's sickness will not end in death. No, it happened for the glory of God so that the Son of God will receive glory from this" (John 11:4, NLT). Jesus stayed where He was for two more days.

By the time Jesus met Martha near their home in Bethany, Lazarus had been dead for four days. Martha said to Jesus, "Lord, if only You had been here, my brother would not have died." Jesus told Martha, "Your brother will rise again." Martha replied, "Yes, in the resurrection." That is when Jesus responded, *"I am the resurrection and the life,"* letting Martha know He is the source of all life and has the power to overcome death.

Still grieving, Mary and Martha took Jesus to the tomb where Lazarus lay. Upon arriving, He was so moved by Lazarus' condition and the sadness Mary and Martha were feeling that tears streamed down Jesus' face.

He ordered the stone removed and said, *"Didn't I tell you that you would see God's glory if you believe?"* (John 11:40, NLT).

Jesus stepped toward the cave's opening and yelled, "Lazarus, come out!" Lazarus, wrapped in burial cloth, stumbled out of the tomb, once dead for four days and now very much alive. Jesus commanded they take off his grave clothes and set him free. In that moment, Jesus demonstrated His power over death and His ability to give spiritual and physical life.

It's Not Over

"I am the living one. I died, but look — I am alive forever and ever! And I hold the keys of death and the grave."
REVELATION 1:18 (NLT)

Two thousand years ago, when the soldiers crucified Jesus, Satan thought it was over — he had finally finished Him off. Satan and all the demons were probably throwing a huge party, giving high-fives, with confetti raining down. They believed they had killed Jesus and gotten rid of Him once and for all.

But Jesus said, "Hold the celebration, blow out the candles, stop the confetti — I've got an announcement to make. Kingdom of darkness, it's not over. I died, but check this out — I'm still alive. You think you've won, but you've got another thing coming."

Jesus declared, *"I am the living one. I died, but look — I am alive forever and ever!"*

Because He lives, we can live. The same power that raised Jesus from the grave lives inside you and me. You're not weak, you're not lacking — you're full of resurrection power. No obstacle is too big, no sickness too great, no enemy too powerful, and no dream too big. The greatest force in the universe is inside of you.

No matter what comes your way, you can have the attitude: It's not over. The enemy may hit you with his best shot, but his best will never be enough. When it's all said and done, you will still be standing strong.

I met a twelve-year-old boy in Chicago named Daniel. One day, he was out playing and having fun like a normal child, and then his whole world collapsed. He was rushed to the hospital and diagnosed with an aggressive brain tumor. The doctors performed emergency surgery to try to save his life. When he woke up, he had lost all his motor skills. Half of his body was paralyzed. He couldn't speak, walk, or feed himself. It looked like it was over.

From the time he was very young, he and his family would watch our television broadcast every Sunday. All through the week, he'd play my messages — a little boy, hearing these words of life over and over: "You're a victor, not a victim. No weapon formed

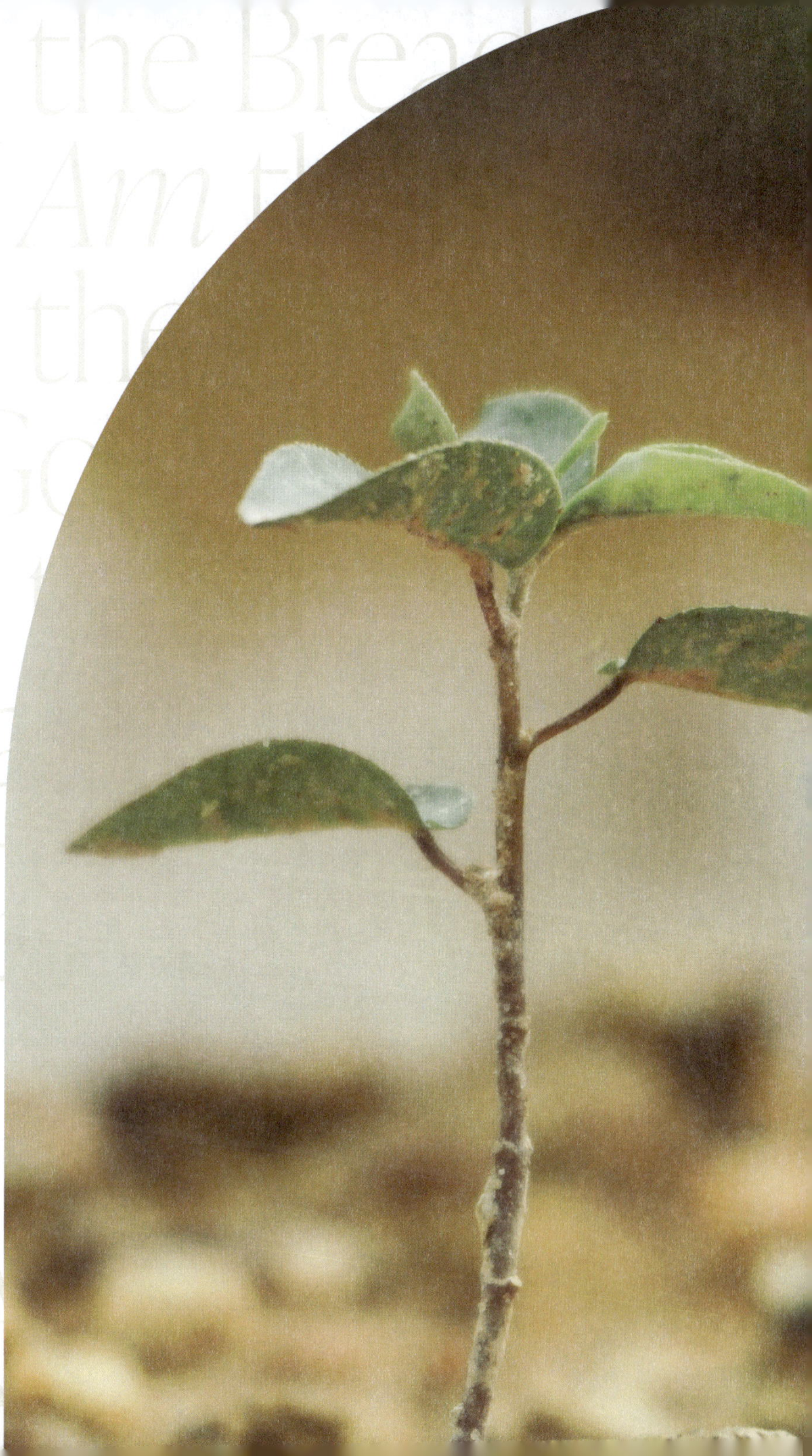

PROMISE: You have life, victory, and unshakable hope, even when everything seems against you. He is the Living One, and because He lives, you have His strength and power to overcome.

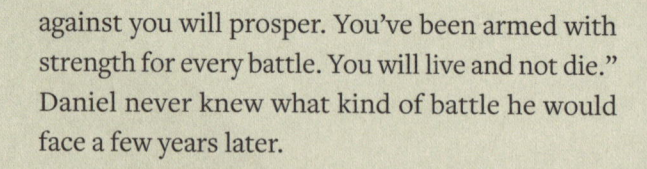

against you will prosper. You've been armed with strength for every battle. You will live and not die." Daniel never knew what kind of battle he would face a few years later.

Daniel spent one hundred days in the hospital. Over the months that followed, he had to relearn how to talk and how to walk. His mother had to quit her job to take care of him, and his father missed three months of work. The chemotherapy and radiation constantly made him sick. Life threw him a curveball. He could have become bitter; he could have given up — but not Daniel. He had faith in the Living God. He'd send me notes thanking me for the messages, and he'd draw pictures with my sayings on them.

You may be up against a major obstacle or facing something that seems broken or dying. But nothing is too hard for the One who is the resurrection and the life. He made your body, and He can correct what's wrong and broken. The medical report may not look good, but God has another report. It says He is restoring health to you. It says with long life He will satisfy you. He has the final say — He says it's not over.

The Champion

He canceled the record of the charges against us and took it away by nailing it to the cross. In this way, he disarmed the spiritual rulers and authorities. He shamed them publicly by his victory over them on the cross.
COLOSSIANS 2:14–15 (NLT)

When Jesus died, they put Him in the tomb on that dark Friday and thought it was the end. I imagine Satan and his forces celebrated their supposed victory with great joy. But on Sunday morning, in the midst of their celebration, they probably heard footsteps getting closer and closer. They see a figure approaching — someone they can't identify. Everyone is accounted for, so who could this be?

The figure walks with confidence and authority they've never encountered before. His eyes blaze like fire, His hair is white like wool, and His face shines like the sun, causing them to turn away. He crashes their party and declares, *"I'm back. You thought you got rid of Me, but I'm here to purchase mankind. Oh, and by the way, you didn't take My life — I gave it away."*

In that moment, Jesus defeated the enemy. He took the keys of death and hell. He dragged Satan through the corridors so all the forces of darkness could see him dethroned, demoralized, and powerless. Jesus paralyzed him and rendered him

PROMISE:
Jesus' resurrection power has conquered and defeated Satan for me, and He now holds the keys to life and death.

impotent. He shamed him publicly by parading him around as a spectacle.

This was the battle of the ages: Good versus evil, light versus darkness, Jesus versus Satan. It was no contest. Jesus easily crushed Satan's head and completely defeated him. He took them captive and paraded them around in a triumphal procession (Colossians 2:15).

In ancient times, when a king conquered a city, he would parade the defeated king through the streets — beaten, battered, soiled, and stained, stripped of royal garments — before all his people, ensuring that everyone knew who the victor was. That's what Jesus did. He made sure that every force of darkness saw Satan with his head bruised, defeated, and powerless.

You Have Power Over Satan

"Listen carefully: I have given you authority [that you now possess] to tread on serpents and scorpions, and [the ability to exercise authority] over all the power of the enemy (Satan); and nothing will [in any way] harm you."
LUKE 10:19 (AMP)

On Sunday morning the grave could hold Jesus no longer. He came bursting out, declaring, "I am He who lives; I was dead, but behold, I am alive forever." He added, "I've got the keys to death and hell."

Then He turned to His followers and said, "I have given you power over all the power of the enemy."

There is an authority Jesus has given to His disciples over spiritual forces of evil. Serpents and scorpions are not snakes and bugs; they are evil spiritual powers. Jesus imparted to you authority to trample demonic powers or spiritual opposition. You have dominion over harmful spiritual forces, and they are under your feet.

PROMISE:

Jesus has given me His resurrection power over the enemy.

With this authority, no power of the enemy can ultimately harm you. We as believers, are safe and protected under God's authority and power. Jesus has empowered you to stand strong against all the spiritual attacks and deceptions of the enemy. The phrase *"nothing will harm you"* (Luke 10:19, NIV) tells us the divine protection believers can confidently walk in as they exercise the authority given to them by Jesus.

The life Jesus brings through His resurrection overcomes all evil powers, including Satan. We as believers not only share in His resurrection life but also in His authority over the powers of darkness. They are assured that they can live victoriously, protected from ultimate harm by the power of God.

The same power He had, He gave us. Now, you and I have all power — it's resurrection power. After all Christ has done, don't you dare go around feeling weak, intimidated, or disadvantaged. Jesus *"disarmed the powers and authorities, he made a public spectacle of them, triumphing over them by the cross"* (Colossians 2:15, NIV). He brought Satan to naught. Another word for naught is zero.

He is a Zero

For He was indeed crucified in weakness, yet He lives by God's power. And though we are weak in Him, yet by God's power we will live with Him to serve you.
2 CORINTHIANS 13:4 (BSB)

When thoughts of fear, worry, doubt, or intimidation come to your mind, don't give in. You live by God's resurrection power. Instead of being afraid or getting negative, give the enemy the big zero sign. You have Jesus, the resurrection and the life, inside of you. Remind him that he has no power over you. When you do, look down because that's where he is — under your feet.

When the thought comes, *You'll never get out of your problem,* put up the zero sign. When the thought says, *Your family is never going to serve God,* put up the zero sign. Instead, say: "As for me and my house, we will serve the Lord." If you hear, "You're never going to accomplish your dreams," raise the zero sign and say, "I can do all things through Christ who strengthens me."

If the enemy whispers, "You're never going to break that addiction," respond with the zero sign. Say, "Whom the Son sets free is free indeed." When the thought says, *You've made too many mistakes,* show the zero sign and say, "God's mercy is bigger than any mistake." Remind the enemy of his defeat.

PROMISE:
I live and move in Christ, my resurrection and life. He has defeated my enemy, and by the authority He has given me, I will overcome.

Joel Osteen

Jesus, You are My Resurrection and Life

Jesus is your resurrection and life over every dead and broken area in your life. Relationships, creative ideas, businesses, lost opportunities, and dying dreams will rise again and thrive. Because Jesus paid the ultimate price by sacrificing His life, you can see these things rise and shine once more.

Don't give up! Put your shoulders back and hold your head high — you are not weak, intimidated, or at a disadvantage. The same resurrection power that raised Christ from the dead lives in you. Your opposition, your enemies, and every intimidating accuser are under your feet. You are above and not beneath. You are the head and not the tail. Because He lives, you will live an abundant, victorious life. I encourage you to walk in resurrection life and thrive.

DECLARATION PRAYER:

Heavenly Father, I thank You for the resurrection power, alive and at work in me. I declare that Jesus is the resurrection and the life, and through Him, I have power over every dead or broken area in my life. By Your authority, I speak to what needs to be restored, and I call forth life in every situation. Just as Lazarus was raised, I declare that what was once thought lost will be made new by Your power.

I proclaim that You have given me authority over all the enemy's power. No weapon formed against me will prosper. I tread upon serpents and scorpions, knowing that I am protected, and nothing can harm me, for I walk in Your divine covering.

Satan is defeated, paralyzed, and rendered powerless. His lies and deceptions hold no power over me because I am more than a conqueror through Christ. When fear, doubt, or intimidation try to rise, declare Jesus is the Victor, and the enemy is under my feet.

I affirm that I carry the same resurrection power that raised Jesus from the dead. I will not walk in weakness or intimidation, for greater is He who is in me than he who is in the world. Every lie, discouraging thought, and attempt to steal my peace is nullified by the authority of Christ in me. In Your mighty name, I declare that I walk in freedom, purpose, and power. I am alive in Christ, and I have victory over every obstacle.

In Jesus' name, amen.

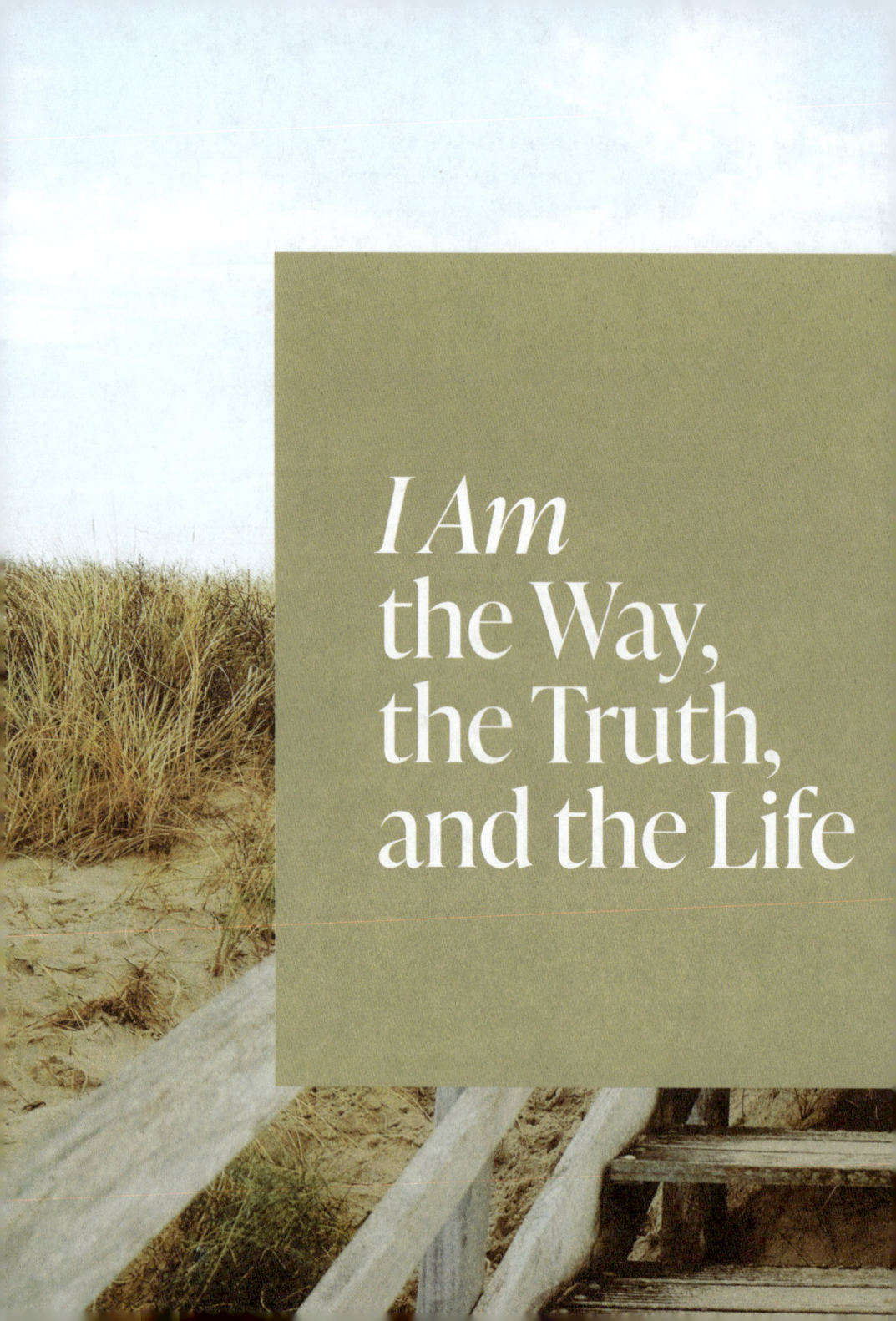

I Am
the Way,
the Truth,
and the Life

Jesus told him, "I am the way, the truth, and the life. No one can come to the Father except through me."

JOHN 14:6 (NLT)

I Am the Way, the Truth, and the Life

Jesus declares Himself the only way to your eternal and abundant life and purpose. He is not only the path to truth but also truth guarding you from the lies of the enemy. Satan desires to steal your identity and distort and deceive you about who you really are. In Jesus, you know who you are. Through Jesus, you have access to His life — His resurrection life. He will restore your life, recover what was lost, restore what was stolen, and heal what was broken.

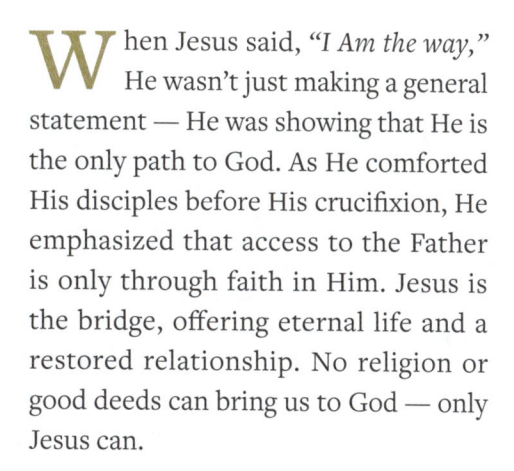

When Jesus said, *"I Am the way,"* He wasn't just making a general statement — He was showing that He is the only path to God. As He comforted His disciples before His crucifixion, He emphasized that access to the Father is only through faith in Him. Jesus is the bridge, offering eternal life and a restored relationship. No religion or good deeds can bring us to God — only Jesus can.

Jesus also called Himself "the truth," meaning He doesn't just teach truth; He embodies it. In a world full of deception, Jesus is the unchanging truth that reveals God's nature and His plan for our salvation. Everything about Him — His life, death, and resurrection — shows us who God truly is.

When Jesus said He is "the life," He meant that He alone gives both physical and eternal life. Believing in Him brings the gift of everlasting life and an abundant life here on earth. Without Him, there's no true life — He is the source and sustainer of it.

Jesus is the only way to salvation, the complete revelation of God's truth, and the giver of eternal life.

Joel Osteen

A Story

In junior high, I was confident and secure and made people laugh. But when I got into high school, all my friends kept growing physically, but I didn't. I started my freshman year at four feet nine inches tall, and people called me "peanut." I began thinking thoughts like, *You're too short. You're at a disadvantage. People are making fun of you.* I let that insecurity in, and it affected my confidence. I became less outgoing and began hiding my personality, growing quieter and more reserved.

When I reached high school, I tried out for the baseball team. I had always been one of the best players in Little League, making the All-Star team every year. But now, in high school, people were bigger and stronger. The coach called out names as we sat in the gym, waiting to hear who made the team. One by one, my friends made it. I kept waiting, but my name wasn't called. The coach eventually pulled me aside and said, "Joel, you're a good player, but you're too small to play at this level."

That was the last thing I needed to hear. I let that moment affect my self-image, confidence, and personality for years. I went into hiding, unsure of myself. I shrank back from opportunities, fearing what people would think and wondering if I was talented enough.

But I could hear God whispering, "Joel, where is the person I created — strong, confident, fun, outgoing?

Why are you shrinking back, letting someone else determine your value, when you have so much more to offer the world?" I had to decide to come out of hiding, stop worrying about what others thought, and not let disappointments steal my passion. I wouldn't be here today if I hadn't made that decision. Jesus is the path to your purpose.

Asking for wisdom, guidance, and instruction is an act of surrender. It takes humility to say, "God, You know what's best for me. I need Your help. I can't do this on my own. Show me the best path."

The Way

Seek His will in all you do, and He will show you which path to take.
PROVERBS 3:6 (NLT)

Too often, we make our plans without consulting God and then ask Him to bless them. Instead, we should ask: "God, is this what You want me to do? Should I start this project, take this trip, or make this purchase?" If you feel peace, go forward; if not, hold off. God knows what's best for us.

Jesus' life and teachings show us how to live in a way that honors God. No matter how uncertain life feels, you're not lost — you have a path to walk, leading to true reality and abundant life.

PROMISE: Jesus will reveal the best path for my life, guiding me with His wisdom and love.

Joel Osteen

PROMISE: Jesus is my way to salvation and the best path for my life.

You need to go to God for direction and listen to what He says — not the negative chatter. God had other plans for me. Despite my talent for baseball, baseball wasn't my future or purpose. God was the way to my future. By seeking Him daily, He has ordered my steps.

As the way for our lives, we must stay closely connected to our Shepherd, following His guidance so we remain on the best path for us.

Identity Theft

"... there is no truth in him. When he lies, it is consistent with his character; for he is a liar and the father of lies."
JOHN 8:44 (NLT)

Jesus is truth, and He desires that we have wisdom and truth inside of us (Psalm 51:6). Satan and his demons, the enemies of our souls, are the opposite of the truth. Jesus exposed His enemy, Satan, by saying, *"... there is no truth in him ... he is a liar and the father of lies"* (John 8:44, NLT).

Satan is a scammer. Being scammed by people can cost us money, time, and effort, but allowing the enemy to deceive you could cost you your destiny. Identity theft may be a widespread issue today, but the greatest identity thief is the enemy of your soul. He knows who you really are — a child of the Most High God, fearfully and wonderfully made.

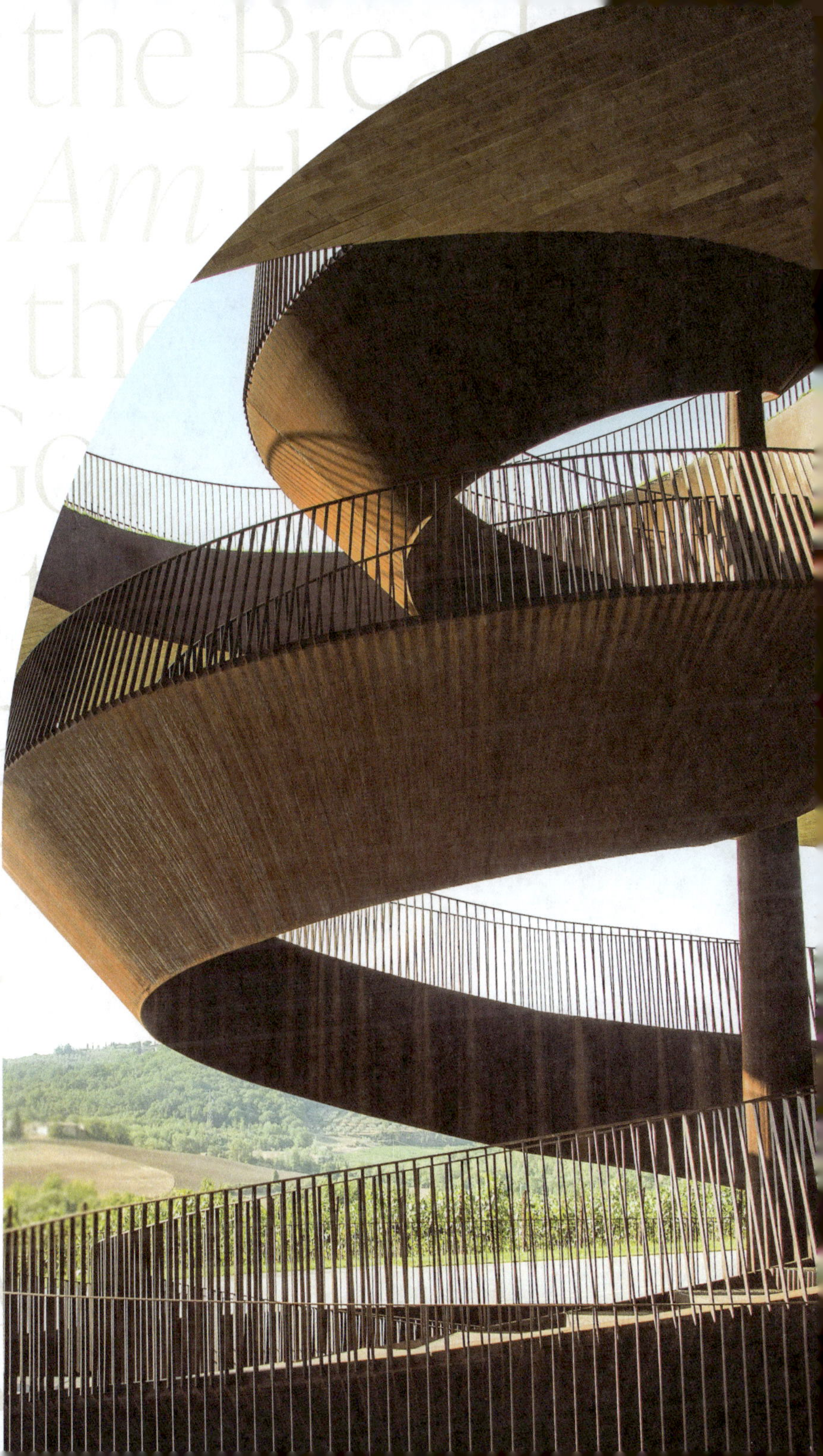

The enemy can see your crown of favor, your robe of righteousness, and the royal blood of Christ flowing through your veins. So, he works to deceive you into believing a lie. He'll whisper, "You're not valuable. You're not attractive. Look at your flaws and weaknesses." If you accept these lies, he'll steal your identity. He'll rob you of the truth of who you are. You're not in a power struggle with the enemy — he's already defeated. Instead, you're in a power struggle with truth. His only power is what you give him by believing his lies.

Scripture tells us to recognize the enemy's schemes and strategies. His two primary weapons are deception and lies. He's subtle and cunning. He doesn't start with an obvious suggestion like, "Steal that money" or "See yourself as worthless." That's too blatant. Instead, he plants a small thought — a seed of doubt. "Your spouse doesn't love you." "It's okay to fudge a little on your taxes." It seems harmless; it's just a suggestion and no big deal. But like clickbait, if you dwell on that thought — if you "click" on it — it opens the door to far more damaging consequences.

The enemy never shows you where those thoughts will lead. He won't tell you that you'll end up broken, lonely, addicted, or discouraged. He's a scammer, and his lies are like clickbait — enticing and appealing at first glance, but by the time you realize you've been scammed, it's too late. Jesus is your path to truth because He embodies truth — what is real. We don't live by what we feel or see because we can be deceived. Besides, we only know in part. But Jesus knows all things, and His Kingdom is what is real. He created us, called us, and empowered us, and He knows the truth about you.

The Scam

"You will know the truth, and the truth will set you free."
JOHN 8:32 (NLT)

The enemy's primary target is your mind. Scripture says that you will know the truth, and the truth will make you free. However, the truth alone won't set you free. It's the truth **you know** that brings freedom. When the enemy plants thoughts of doubt, fear, or compromise, you must return to the truth in God's Word. Answer doubts with faith and lies with the truth of God's promises.

For example, when the thought comes, *You'll never get well; it would have happened by now*, respond with, "No, God is restoring health to me. I will live and not die." If you hear, "You'll never get ahead; everyone in your family struggles," answer with, "I will lend and not borrow. I will prosper and succeed."

The enemy is a scammer. He may be convincing, but you have an advantage: the Spirit of God lives within you. You have the mind of Christ, full of wisdom and discernment. It's helpful to pray,

PROMISE:
Jesus will lead me into truth, and if I walk with Him, I am walking in reality, purpose, and empowerment, free from the enemy's deceptions.

PROMISE:
Jesus will alert you to scams, guide you into truth, and save you from heartache.

"Holy Spirit, I thank You for making me aware of the enemy's schemes, every lie, and every strategy designed to stop my destiny. Help me guard my mind and dismiss and cast down every thought that is against Your will."

Every morning, I pray to Jesus, the truth, for wisdom and discernment — wisdom to make right decisions that honor God and move me toward my destiny. Discernment enables us to see intentions and motives, helping us recognize the source of a thought. When you ask God, He'll help you discern what's right and what's not. That still, small voice inside will alert you to deception. It may look fine; the fruit may seem good, and thoughts might whisper, *It's okay*, but the Spirit of God within you will give you a check or an uneasiness, saying, "It's not right. It's not what it seems."

When you're sensitive to that inward witness and act on it, God will keep you from being scammed. That's Jesus, the Spirit of truth, revealing lies and deception. God will always warn you before you make a mistake. There will be unrest, an uneasiness in your spirit. If you pay attention and act on it, it will save you from heartache.

Fact-Checking

My child, eat honey, for it is good, and the honeycomb is sweet to the taste. In the same way, wisdom is sweet to your soul. If you find it, you will have a bright future, and your hopes will not be cut short.
PROVERBS 24:13–14 (NLT)

We often hear about fact-checking in the media. However, they don't know the truth because they don't know everything Jesus does. It's essential to fact-check the thoughts that enter your mind against God's Word. For example, when thoughts say, *You're not valuable. You're unattractive.* Compare that to the truth found in God's Word: You are a masterpiece created in God's image (Ephesians 2:10). Reject the lie — don't fall for that scam.

When thoughts whisper, *Nothing good is in your future. You've faced too many disappointments — just accept it.* Flag those lies as **false** and **deceptive**. Counter them by fact-checking. Say, "The path of the righteous shines brighter and brighter. God is taking me from glory to glory. I haven't seen, heard, or imagined what God has in store for me."

A friend of mine grew up with two older brothers. Their father was very involved, but he spent more time with her brothers, attending their games and practices. As a young girl, she felt left out. One day, when her family went to a ballgame without her, a thought came: *The reason your father doesn't spend as much time with you is because he never wanted a daughter — he wanted all sons.*

She was only ten years old and didn't know better, so she believed the lie. She began to feel insecure, unworthy, and not valuable. Her personality became more reserved and introverted, and she and her father grew distant. She lived for years with the nagging feeling that she wasn't good enough.

In her forties, her father tragically died in a car accident. After the funeral, she found herself at her grandmother's house, where she was given a box of memorabilia from her father's life. Among the items, she found a letter her father had written to his parents when he was in the army. In it, he said, "Mom and Dad, I can't wait to have a little girl someday. If

I don't get married, I'll adopt a daughter — that's what I want more than anything else."

When she read that letter, she broke down in tears. For years, she believed the lie that her father didn't want her when, in fact, she was his dream. He loved her more than she could have imagined. That one lie as a little girl had affected her entire life, but the truth had been there all along. She shared her story to show how the enemy plants seeds of doubt in our minds. If we don't learn to cast down and reject those lies, they can take root and keep us from fulfilling our destiny.

Jesus embodies the truth about God, humanity, and salvation. Jesus is the ultimate source of truth in a world of confusion and deception. His words and actions reveal God's will and show us how to live in alignment with Him.

Dream Again

"The thief's purpose is to steal and kill and destroy. My purpose is to give them a rich and satisfying life."
JOHN 10:10 (NLT)

One reason Jesus came to earth was to recover what was lost, restore what was stolen, and heal what was broken. Jesus is the giver of life: to give you beauty for ashes, joy for mourning, and to take what was meant for harm and turn it to your advantage.

PROMISE:
God's truth will set you free, guide you, protect you from deception, and lead you to the bright future He has planned for you. The Holy Spirit ensures you can discern lies, overcome doubt, and step into the fullness of your God-given destiny.

Perhaps some things in your life are broken, or your dream has died. Jesus is your resurrection and life. What you've lost is coming back. God is about to do a new thing. He's not going to leave you at a deficit. He sees what you've been through and will make up for it. He will breathe new life, passion, opportunities, and vision into you. You haven't seen the best version of you yet. It's still in front of you.

But there's something you must do. You can't sit on the sidelines, feeling sorry for yourself, thinking you're washed up, guilty. If you think *I've made so many mistakes, why did these people do me wrong?* You will get stuck where you are if you have that defeated mentality. It would be best if you got back in the game. Stir your faith up. Start believing again. Start dreaming again. Start hoping again.

Jesus is your path to truth and a good life. God's Word and the Holy Spirit will guide you and give you wisdom and protection. The enemy's primary tactic is to attack the mind with lies, fear, and deception, but through knowing and embracing God's truth, we find freedom. It is the truth we personally know and apply that brings freedom to our lives.

God's Word and His promises are our defense against the enemy's lies. When doubt or fear arises, you should answer with the truths found in Scripture, such as promises of healing, prosperity, and a bright future. The enemy can plant deceptive thoughts from an early age. Those unchecked lies can steal our confidence and destiny if we don't recognize and reject them.

We can recognize the enemy's schemes and avoid deception by praying for discernment and truth. You're promised divine guidance in your decisions and assured that God will give you a warning or a "check" in your spirit when something isn't right. Ultimately, through God's truth, His Word, and His Spirit, we are led to a brighter future filled with purpose and the fulfillment of His promises.

Guard your mind. Keep it filled with faith, hope, and victory. If you do this, I believe and declare that every stronghold will come down and every wrong mindset will be broken. You have the Spirit of wisdom and discernment within you. You will rise higher, accomplish your dreams, and become all you were created to be, in Jesus' name.

PROMISE:
Jesus will restore your life, recover what was lost, restore what was stolen, and heal what was broken.

Jesus, You are My Way, Truth, and Life

Jesus is your direct path to a deep, personal relationship with God. He offers you access to the Father, guiding you in truth and giving you eternal life. By placing your faith in Him, you receive not only the assurance of life after death but also abundant life here and now, filled with His presence, purpose, and peace. Jesus is your way to fulfillment, your source of truth in a confusing world, and the One who sustains your life, both physically and spiritually.

DECLARATION PRAYER:

Heavenly Father, I confidently come before You, knowing that You have called and created me for a divine purpose. Today, I declare that every lie of the enemy will be exposed and defeated. I cast down every thought of fear, doubt, and compromise that seeks to steal my joy and derail my destiny. I stand on Your truth, knowing that it's not just the truth but the truth I know that sets me free.

I declare your Word that I have the mind of Christ. The Spirit of wisdom and discernment lives within me, guiding my steps and helping me recognize the enemy's schemes. Every strategy, every stronghold, and every lie is being broken right now in the name of Jesus. I dismiss deception and embrace Your truth.

Lord, You have given me a spirit of hope, victory, and faith. I declare that I will rise higher, overcome every challenge, and walk in the fullness of the purpose You have set for me. No weapon formed against me will prosper, and every thought that contradicts Your Word will be cast down. I align my heart and mind with Your promises, believing that You are taking me from glory to glory.

I am Your masterpiece, created with love and intention. My future is bright because You, my way, truth, and life are with me. I will fulfill my destiny, I will live in victory, and I will see Your goodness in my life.

In Jesus' mighty name, I pray. Amen.

I Am the Vine

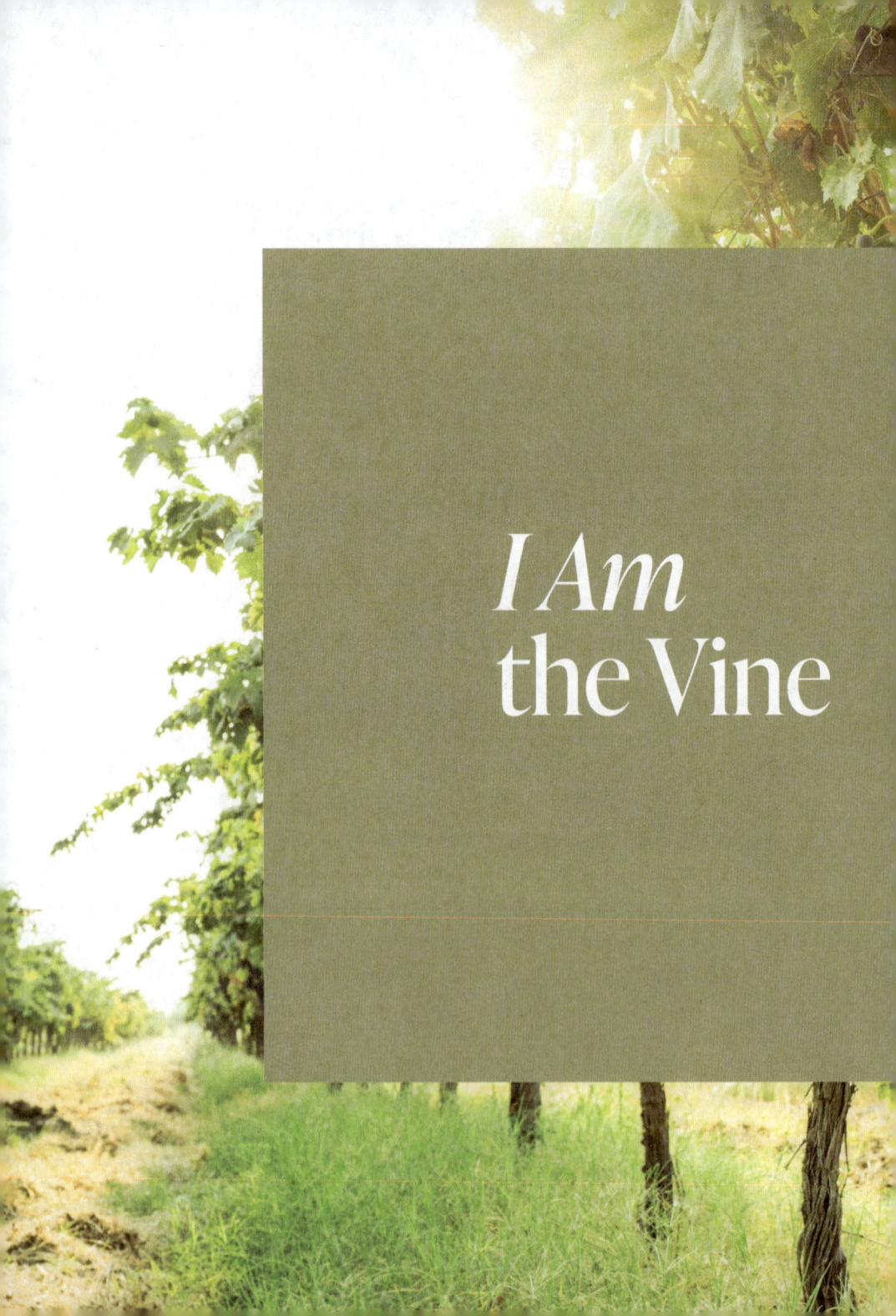

"Yes, I am the vine; you are the branches. Those who remain in me, and I in them, will produce much fruit. For apart from me you can do nothing."

JOHN 15:5 (NLT)

I Am the Vine

Jesus is the source of your spiritual vitality, and as His followers, we must remain connected to Him to bear fruit. True spiritual growth and productivity come from a continuous relationship with Jesus. Without Him, our efforts will be fruitless, but with Him, there is the potential for abundant growth and purpose.

Abiding in Christ requires intentionality and dependence on Him. Through prayer, reading His Word, obeying His commands, relying on the Holy Spirit, staying in fellowship, and being open to God's pruning, you can experience the fullness of life Jesus offers. As you remain connected to the True Vine, your life will bear much fruit for His glory.

The vine and branches illustrate the vital connection between Christ and His followers. Just as branches depend on the vine for life, we rely on Jesus for spiritual growth, purpose, and positive impact. Cultivating an ongoing relationship through faith, prayer, and obedience enables us to bear "fruit" — good works, spiritual growth, and influence. Without this connection to Christ, lasting spiritual results are impossible.

David's Story

As a teenager, David spent his days in the shepherd's fields, faithfully tending to his father's sheep. God had placed a big dream in David's heart, and though he knew he was destined for greatness, he found himself isolated, unnoticed, and seemingly stuck tending sheep in the fields. It wasn't like he was climbing a ladder, gaining recognition or opportunities to prove himself. He could have easily become frustrated, thinking, *I'm made for more than this. I must get out there and show people what I can do.*

David didn't rush to make something happen outside of God's timing. Instead, he stayed faithful in the shepherd's fields, diligently caring for the sheep, ensuring their safety, and that they were well-fed, even when no one else was watching. In those quiet moments, David would take his harp and sing to God, pouring out his heart in worship. Through these times of solitude, David built a deep, personal relationship with the Lord, trusting Him with his future.

What David was doing during that time was abiding — remaining connected to God, trusting in His plan. David's heart was saying, "God, I trust You. I believe You will open the right doors and get me to my destiny."

One day, everything changed. God had told the prophet Samuel to anoint one of Jesse's sons as the next king of Israel. Samuel came to David's house and looked at all seven sons that were presented to him, but none of them were the ones God had chosen. Jesse had to send a messenger to bring David in from the fields, where he had faithfully abided. As soon as Samuel saw David, he knew — this was the one.

David didn't seek out the crown; the crown came to him. David didn't manipulate circumstances, grow bitter about his time in the fields, or complain about being overlooked. Instead, he remained faithful, doing his best when no one was watching. And because he abided, his destiny came knocking at his door.

Interestingly, after Samuel anointed David as king, instead of claiming the throne, David excused himself and went back to tending sheep. Even though Saul was still the reigning king, David understood that the timing wasn't right. He went back to abiding, trusting in God's plan, and staying connected to the vine. This shows that David's heart was pure, and his motives were in line with God's will. Over time he had every opportunity and even the right to overthrow Saul and take his place as ruler of Israel, but he chose not to. On two occasions, David declared, "I will not touch the Lord's anointed," demonstrating his deep respect for God's timing and authority.

Abiding

"If you abide in Me, and My words abide in you, you will ask what you desire, and it shall be done for you. By this My Father is glorified, that you bear much fruit; so you will be My disciples."
JOHN 15:7–8 (NKJV)

Jesus paints a beautiful picture of the relationship between Himself and His followers using the metaphor of a vine and branches. Just as branches must stay connected to the vine to produce fruit, believers must remain connected to Jesus to live fruitful and meaningful spiritual lives.

Jesus said that if we abide in Him, we will bear much fruit. In this passage, He speaks of fruit, more fruit, and much fruit. The way to increase, to move to the next level, is simply by abiding. Jesus taught us that when life doesn't make sense — when we face things we don't understand, when we could easily grow bitter or lose heart — if we choose to trust Him, we will bear fruit.

When you keep doing your best, believe He is still directing your steps, praise Him in unfair circumstances, and remain faithful when you could be frustrated, you are abiding. To abide means continuing to do the right thing: serving, giving, smiling, expecting His favor, and going the extra mile. These are the moments that prove your faithfulness, and they lead to greater fruit.

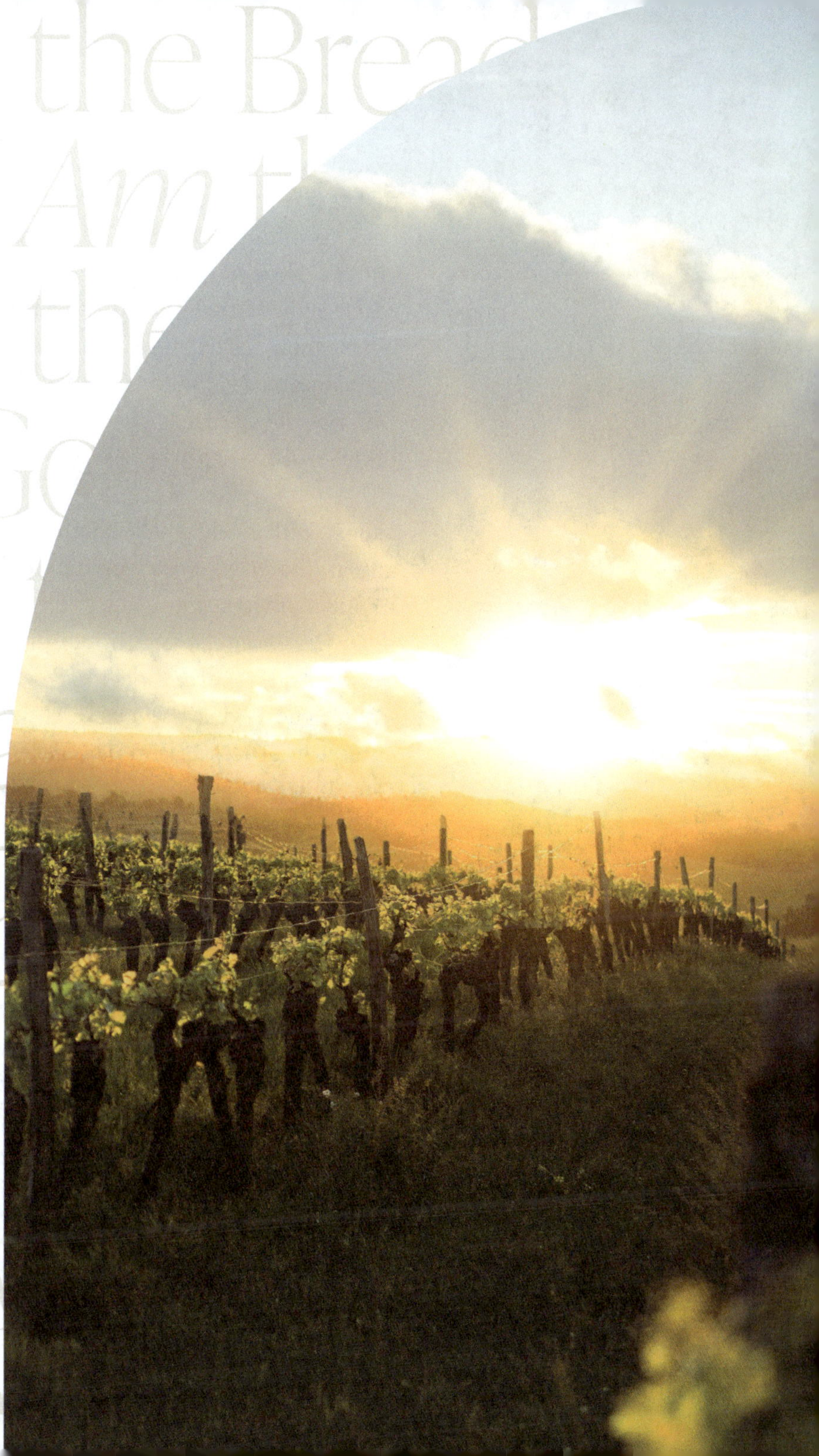

When you show God that you will be faithful during seasons of cutback, He will release you into seasons of much fruit. He will take you to places you could never reach on your own. But before reaching new levels, we must go through seasons where things are stripped away, life feels uncomfortable, and what worked before no longer works. Don't be discouraged. That cutback season is part of the process — preparing you for new growth.

I spoke with a man whose company had been sold, and all the employees were let go. He struggled to find a job for a long time and eventually had to move back home, living with his mother in his fifties. He said, "I never thought I'd be here at my age. I don't know what happened." I told him he had entered a cutback season. This wasn't a surprise to God. Whether he stayed in that season or moved forward depended on how he responded.

If you get bitter, complain, focus on how unfair life is, and walk around defeated, you'll get stuck. But when you realize that the cutback is a sign of new growth, that more fruit is in your future, and that God is preparing you for new levels, everything changes. If you choose to thank Him, believe He's in control, and go around being kind to others, things will turn in your favor. You'll see new doors open.

I saw him again about six months later. He had a new job and had moved into a new house. He said, "I'm happier and more fulfilled than I've ever been." Saying, "God, I don't understand it, but I trust You. I know You wouldn't have allowed this if You didn't have a purpose. I want to thank You that I'm not just going to come out of this; I'm going to come out better."

Like David, when you stay faithful in the quiet seasons, when you abide in God even when nothing seems to be happening, favor will come looking for you. The right opportunities, good breaks, healing, and the people you need will show up at your door. God hasn't forgotten about you. He sees your faithfulness, even when it's hard, and your time is coming. Stay connected to the vine, and know that something extraordinary — better than you imagined — is on the way. The delay isn't because you've been forgotten; it's because God has something bigger in store than you ever expected.

Stop Striving

"Be still, and know that I am God! I will be honored by every nation. I will be honored throughout the world."
PSALM 46:10 (NLT)

One translation says, *"Stop striving and know that I am God"* (NASB). As long as you're trying to fix everything and thinking it's all up to you, you won't truly experience God's favor. It's freeing to realize that you don't have to make everything happen.

PROMISE:
God uses seasons of difficulty and loss to prepare you for greater growth, fruitfulness, and new levels, as long as you remain faithful and trust in His plan.

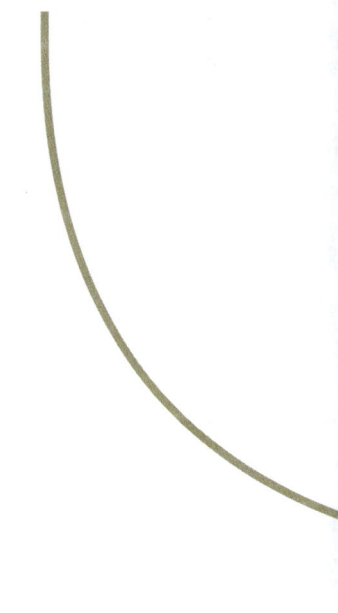

PROMISE:
Trust God and rest in Him. He will handle what you can't, bringing favor, peace, and fruitful outcomes into your life.

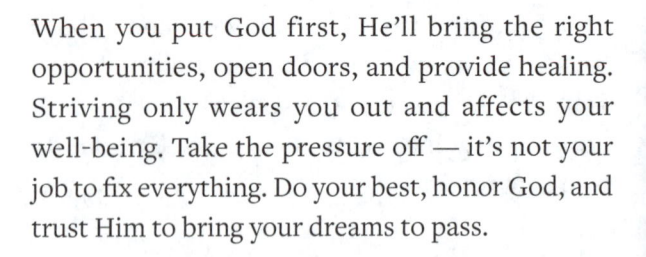

When you put God first, He'll bring the right opportunities, open doors, and provide healing. Striving only wears you out and affects your well-being. Take the pressure off — it's not your job to fix everything. Do your best, honor God, and trust Him to bring your dreams to pass.

Jesus said, *"I am the vine; you are the branches. Whoever abides in me and I in him, he it is that bears much fruit, for apart from me you can do nothing"* (John 15:5, ESV). Abiding means to depend, rely, and rest in Him. When you stop striving and trust God, you'll naturally bear fruit, and He will make things happen that you couldn't achieve on your own.

The word "abide" means to depend, to rely on, and to rest. Jesus was saying, "If you depend on Me and rest in Me, you can relax." You don't have to strive, force things to happen, live worried, or feel pressured about how it will all come together. When you're abiding in Him (resting in), you will naturally bear much fruit.

Jesus said, *"Apart from me you can do nothing"* (v. 5, NIV). Imagine Jesus is about to leave His disciples and gives them the secret to their mission: "This is how you will be successful; this is how you'll overcome challenges; this is how you'll fulfill your destiny: abide in Me, and you will bear much fruit."

Best Prayer

One of the best prayers we can pray each morning is, "God, I'm depending on You today. I'm relying on You, and I'm going to rest in You. I believe that I will bear much fruit because I'm connected to You."

This doesn't mean we sit back and do nothing. We still need to use our gifts and do our best, but we shouldn't rely solely on our abilities, thinking we must make everything happen. Do what you can, then leave the rest to God. As long as you're abiding in Him, you won't just bear a little fruit, but much fruit.

When someone says, "Aren't you worried about your child? He's not getting better." Say, "No, I'm not worrying — I'm abiding. I'm trusting and believing, and I know God's in control." If you lose a big contract and someone asks, "Aren't you upset?" say, "No, I know I'm connected to the vine, to a supply line that never runs dry. I won't live stressed — I'm abiding and at peace. I know another opportunity is coming." When faced with a bad medical report, say, "Yes, but I'm not moved by what I see — I'm moved by what I know. God is restoring health to me. I'm depending on Him, relying on Him, and I'm relaxing, knowing nothing can snatch me out of His hands."

PROMISE:
By depending on God and staying connected to Him, you will experience peace and abundant blessings, knowing that He will guide you through every challenge.

Joel Osteen

Lemons

"Yes, I am the vine; you are the branches. Those who remain in me, and I in them, will produce much fruit. For apart from me you can do nothing."
JOHN 15:5 (NLT)

We have lemon trees in our backyard, and I see the lemons hanging on the vine. They're simply abiding, not struggling or frustrated. They don't think, "Why am I not growing faster? How will I change from green to yellow? What if I don't ripen?" I've never heard a lemon complain or seen one look worried. They hang there, drawing strength from the vine, confident that they'll get everything they need as long as they're connected to the source.

Sometimes, we worry about how to achieve our dreams, whether we'll meet the right people, or if we'll get opportunities like a scholarship. But as long as you're connected to the vine, you don't have to stress. It's not your job to figure everything out. Just like lemons can't see everything happening within them — getting nutrients, developing pulp, and growing seeds — the same is true for us. We're the fruit, not the vine. The vine provides everything needed for our growth and development.

God promised Abraham and Sarah a child, but instead of abiding and trusting in His timing, they grew impatient and decided to take matters into their own hands. Sarah urged Abraham to have a child with her maid, leading to the birth of Ishmael, but this was not the promised child and caused significant strife. It's better to wait for what's right than to settle for something born out of impatience and effort.

If your promise hasn't come to pass yet, trust that God knows what's best and keep abiding, doing the right thing. Even if you've made mistakes and forced things in the past, God's promise remains. Twenty-five years after the promise, Sarah gave birth to Isaac, the promised child, despite their impatience and mistakes. It just may take longer than expected, but don't settle for less.

Use your gifts, do what you can, but don't force outcomes. Keep abiding in God; in due time, you'll see His promises fulfilled in your life. In the meantime, relax and enjoy the present, staying close to God for the strength, favor, and blessings you need.

Pruning

"I am the true grapevine, and my Father is the gardener. He cuts off every branch of mine that doesn't produce fruit, and he prunes the branches that do bear fruit so they will produce even more."
JOHN 15:1–2 (NLT)

When things in our lives are unproductive — such as a friend pulling us down, time wasted on the computer, or a stagnant job — hold us back, God will cut them away so we can focus our energy on

PROMISE:
As long as you stay connected to God, He will provide everything you need for growth and success.

what truly moves us forward. Losing something that isn't adding value can be understandable, but in John 15, Jesus says that every branch that does bear fruit, the gardener cuts back so it will bear more fruit. To progress from bearing fruit to bearing more fruit, a cutback is necessary.

Sometimes, losing things that don't make sense can be discouraging, especially when you're working with a good attitude, helping others, and faithfully doing what's right, only to face setbacks. Instead of becoming disheartened or losing passion, recognize it as a pruning season. Without this cutback, new growth won't occur. God is not satisfied with you staying where you are; He has greater things in store for you — new levels, opportunities, and relationships. Will you trust Him during these pruning times? Will you continue to do the right thing even when it feels like things are going backward and you're tempted to be discouraged?

I believe in standing against sickness, addictions, and dysfunction, but not every difficulty comes from the enemy. Sometimes, it's the Gardener at work. God prunes us — not to limit us, but to prepare us for new growth. If you're discouraged by something you've lost or a situation that hasn't worked out, it might be God's hand, not the enemy, shaping your path. We often give the enemy too much credit; he can't touch you without God's permission.

Your praise during pruning seasons carries more weight than during harvest seasons. It shows that you trust God and that He is working within you — developing your character and strengthening your spiritual muscles. While we might not like the cutbacks, God, the Gardener, knows exactly when and where to prune. He won't take away what you need or cut something back without giving you more. The enemy hasn't seized control of the pruning shears; God is still in charge. Even if the cutbacks don't make sense, that's what faith is all about. Dare to trust Him.

If you're in a pruning season with discouraging setbacks, recognize that God is positioning you for greater fruit. He wouldn't prune you if something better weren't on the horizon. Keep abiding, thanking Him, and maintaining a faith-filled attitude. I believe and declare that this loss is not permanent. You are about to experience much fruit. New doors will open, new relationships will come, and negative situations will turn around. Because you abide in Him, abundance, healing, breakthroughs, and new levels of your destiny are on their way, in Jesus' name.

PROMISE:
As you trust in God's pruning and abide in Him, He will guide you through challenges to greater growth, abundant fruitfulness, and new levels of blessings and favor.

Jesus, You are My Vine

Today can be a turning point. Release the pressure and accept that you can't fix everyone or change everything; that's not your job. God tells you what He said thousands of years ago: "Stop striving, be still, and you will know I am God." If you choose to abide instead of strive, I believe and declare that not only will you enjoy your life more, but you will also bear much fruit. The promotion will come looking for you — unexpected blessings, healing, restoration, the right people, favor, and new levels of your destiny — because you are connected to the vine.

DECLARATION PRAYER:

Heavenly Father, today, I come before You full of faith and trust. I declare that You are the true Gardener of my life, and I fully rely on You. I acknowledge that in times of pruning, it may not be the enemy, but Your loving hand is guiding me. I trust that Your pruning is not to limit me but to prepare me for greater growth and fruitfulness.

Lord, I release the pressure to fix everything and to make things happen on my own. I embrace Your promise that I will bear much fruit as I abide in You. Help me to be patient, keep my focus on You, and trust Your timing. I choose to be still and know that You are God, believing that You control every situation in my life.

Father, I declare that my current challenges and setbacks are not permanent. Healing, restoration, new opportunities, the right relationships, and favor are coming into my life. I trust that You are bringing me to new levels of my destiny, and I am confident that abundance and breakthroughs are on the horizon.

I thank You, Lord, for the growth You cultivate in me and the fruit that will come from abiding in You. I commit to doing my part — doing what is right, and maintaining an attitude of gratitude. In Jesus' name, I declare that this is a turning point. I trust in Your plan and anticipate the blessings and new levels You have prepared for me.

In Jesus' name, amen.

I Am
the Alpha
and the
Omega

"I am the Alpha and the Omega, the First and the Last, the Beginning and the End."

REVELATION 22:13 (NIV)

I Am the Alpha and the Omega

Jesus is the Beginning and the End, seeing the entire scope of your life. Because He exists outside of time, He positions events and aligns circumstances to fulfill His will as we follow Him in obedience.

Jesus is both the source and the fulfillment of all things — the One who created us and ultimately draws us to Himself. As the Alpha and Omega, He sees the full scope of your life and knows the exact moment for each part of His plan to unfold.

God's timing and promises are flawless. He knows what is best for you because He sees the entire picture — from beginning to end.

When you face uncertainty, challenges, or even success, you can find comfort knowing that He holds everything together. His eternal nature assures that nothing happens outside of His knowledge or power, giving you peace and confidence to rely on Him in every season.

Joel Osteen

The Faith of Mary

Mary, a young teenager living in Nazareth, appeared to be favored and had so much going for her, yet at the same time, many things also seemed to go wrong. She was engaged to be married to a righteous man named Joseph and was excited, eagerly planning the wedding. She felt blessed to be engaged to such a devout man, and it was one of the happiest times of her life.

Then, an angel appeared to Mary, telling her that she would conceive a child by the Holy Spirit and that the child would be the Messiah. Mary was amazed — out of all the women in the world, she had been chosen to carry Jesus. However, the angel did not warn her of the many challenges that were about to happen before the promise was fulfilled. She found herself in a difficult situation — pregnant before marriage.

Joseph was unconvinced when Mary shared the news with him, explaining that the child was not from another man but from the Holy Spirit. Deeply hurt and confused, Joseph was ready to break off the engagement. He couldn't bear the thought of being embarrassed or humiliated by his fiancée having a child that wasn't his.

The angel had to visit Joseph, saying, "I know this seems wrong and unusual, but Mary is telling the truth. Stay with her." Meanwhile, people in the town began gossiping: "Look at her — pregnant and not even married!" Slander and hurtful talk surrounded them — yet another challenge.

Nine months later, just as Mary was about to give birth, King Herod called for a census, requiring everyone to travel to Bethlehem. It was terrible timing. Mary was exhausted, unable to sleep, her feet swollen, and her back aching. *And Joseph, you want me to travel ninety miles on a donkey, bouncing up and down?* she must have thought.

When they finally arrived in Bethlehem late at night, Joseph went to an inn and asked for a room. The innkeeper replied, "Sorry, no room tonight. We're full." Joseph pleaded, "My wife's about to have a baby. We've traveled a long way." But the answer remained, "Sorry, we have nothing." Another closed door — yet another wrong. Joseph eventually found a cave where animals were kept — the only place available. Mary gave birth to Jesus and laid Him in a cow's trough.

We often see the Christmas card image of this beautiful scene: Mary smiling with baby Jesus, the wise men standing nearby, and the star glowing overhead. It looks so peaceful and glorious.

But if Mary could speak to us, she would say, "Yes, it was a glorious night, and yes, I am honored to have been the mother of Christ, but there are many things you didn't see that went wrong that I had to endure to get there. I became pregnant at the wrong time. My fiancé wanted to leave me. People tried to ruin my reputation. I had to travel on a donkey while very pregnant. Then, I had to give birth in a cattle stall. But all of those wrongs were part of God's plan. If I hadn't been faithful through the wrongs, I wouldn't have made it to the right."

When facing wrongs in your life, remember this: God has graced you for everything you'll face. He won't allow a wrong without giving you the strength, favor, and endurance to overcome it. Don't complain. Don't say, "Why did this happen? It's too much. It's not fair." Instead, stay strong because you are well-able. You've been equipped and empowered for every season.

Isaiah prophesied that a virgin would conceive (Isaiah 7:14), so Mary had to become pregnant, even at what seemed like the wrong time. It was prophesied that Jesus was to be born in Bethlehem (Micah 5:2), so Herod's census — coming at a time that seemed wrong — was necessary to move Mary and Joseph from Nazareth to Bethlehem. All of these wrongs were necessary.

Let me tell you: there is a prophecy over your life, too. God has already ordained things for you to accomplish, written in His book before time began. He is the beginning and the end. He knows and sees it all. Like Mary, you may not understand everything that happens. It may feel wrong, unfair, or poorly timed, but it's all part of His plan.

Am the Bread
ife I Am t
Am the
he Go
Am t
on a
m t
ruth
Am
he A
ome

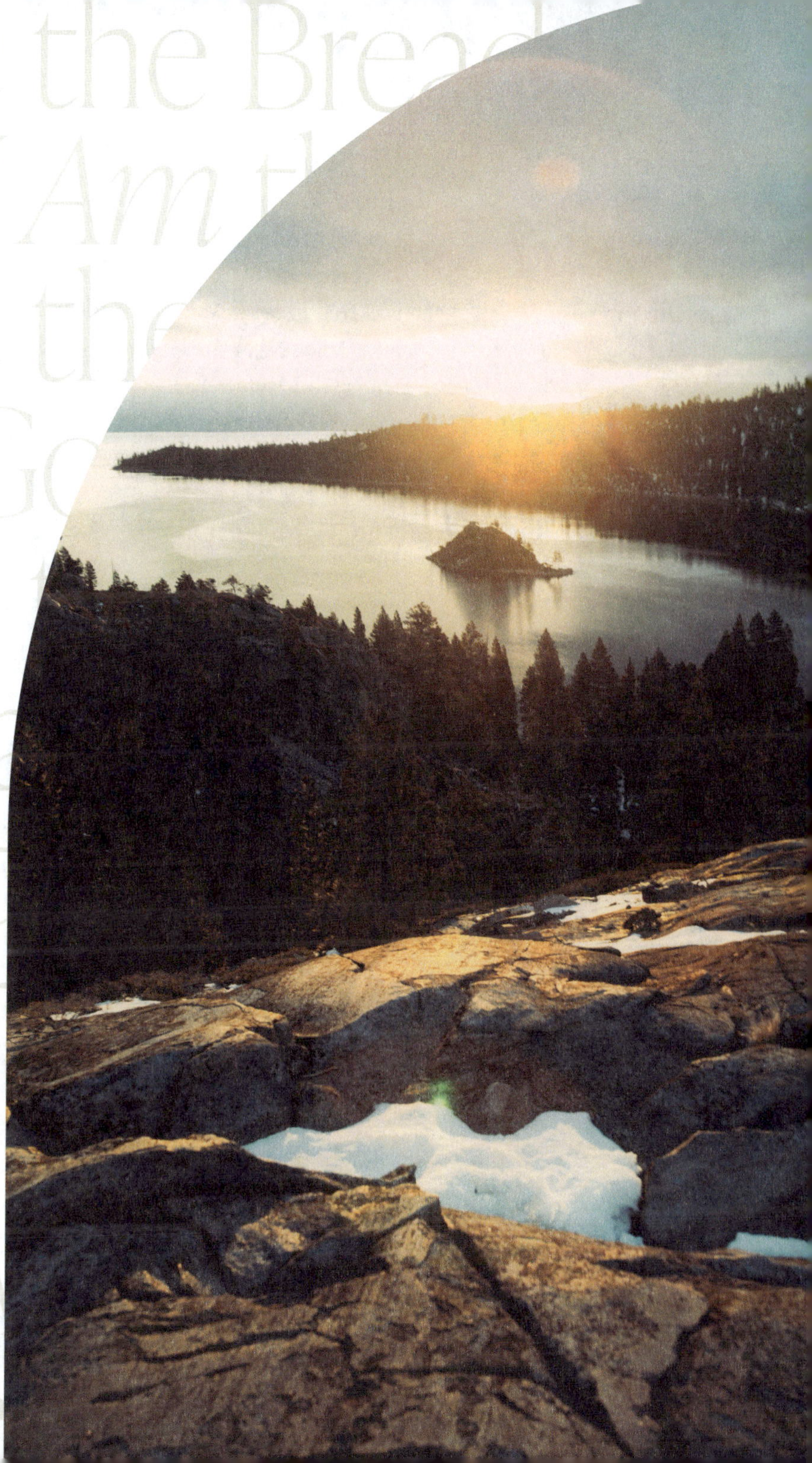

PROMISE: God's plans for you will prevail despite the challenges and "wrongs" you encounter. The difficulties we face are not setbacks but are set ups, essential parts of His purpose, leading us to fulfill His greater promises in our lives.

You must go through the wrongs before you get to the right. God may give you a promise or a dream, but if you don't know how to handle the wrongs or realize that these wrongs are part of His plan, you might get discouraged and give up. The Alpha and Omega is at the beginning and end of your life. He is God and there is no other. He makes known the end from the beginning and His purposes will stand (Isaiah 46:9–10).

The Right Time

> *"Is anything too hard for the LORD? I will return about this time next year, and Sarah will have a son."*
> **GENESIS 18:14 (NLT)**

Abraham and Sarah initially struggled to believe they could have a baby. They doubted and questioned, "How can this happen?" God responded, "You may doubt and not see how, but I have already set the right time." At the appointed time, Sarah would give birth. Notice that God established the timing when He made the promise.

Whatever God has promised you, He has already set the right time. It's already in your future. The question is: What do we do when the fulfillment seems delayed? God's timing isn't always our timing. On the journey to your promise being fulfilled, you might face opportunities to become discouraged and give up. You may think, *If it were going to happen, it would have happened by now.* That's when you need to dig deep and declare, "God, I trust You. I know You wouldn't have promised this if You didn't have the right timing."

A year passed, and Abraham and Sarah still had no baby. Two years went by, then three, and Sarah remained barren. In their impatience, they made mistakes, attempting to help God. Sarah suggested that Abraham have a child with her maid, which led to the birth of a son, but this was not the promised child. This decision caused strife and division. You don't need to help God or manipulate the situation. It may not happen as quickly as you wish, but trust in God's timing. It's far better to wait for God to work in His way.

Eventually, Abraham and Sarah understood this principle. Romans 4:19–20 says, *"Without weakening in his faith, he faced the fact that his body was as good as dead — since he was about a hundred years old — and that Sarah's womb was also dead. Yet he did not waver through unbelief regarding the promise of God, but was strengthened in his faith and gave glory to God"* (NIV).

They stopped being frustrated and trying to force things and began to believe that their right time was ahead. The Bible says that **at the appointed time,** God would give Sarah a son (Genesis 18:14).

The key is to trust Him while you're waiting. Trust Him as His plan unfolds. Don't be discouraged by

PROMISE:
He knows the beginning from the end and sees the entire scope of your life. He works behind the scenes, aligning everything perfectly according to His plan, even when you cannot see it.

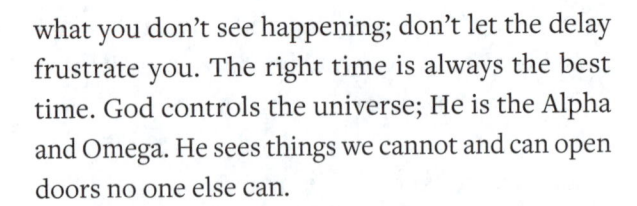

what you don't see happening; don't let the delay frustrate you. The right time is always the best time. God controls the universe; He is the Alpha and Omega. He sees things we cannot and can open doors no one else can.

Trust that your right times are coming. Believe that God has already scheduled your promotion, vindication, breakthroughs, and victories. He will make things happen that you cannot accomplish alone and guide you to your destiny.

Meeting Victoria

A man's mind plans his way [as he journeys through life], but the Lord *directs his steps and establishes them.*
PROVERBS 16:9 (AMP)

In my early twenties, I hadn't dated anyone. Eventually, I got tired of hanging out with the guys and said, "God, I want to meet someone." A few years went by without any change, but I continued to believe that God had the right person lined up for me. I didn't try to force anything; I kept honoring God, doing the right thing, and trusting He was guiding my steps.

One day, the battery in my watch died. My friend Johnny and I were heading to the gym, and I noticed a jewelry store on the way. I decided to stop in for a battery replacement. Out walked the most beautiful girl I had ever seen — Victoria. I didn't mention it to her, but I thought, *God, You've just answered my prayer.*

We started talking, and I found out she was a believer and attended a church like ours across town. I thought, *That's great! If she weren't a believer, I was ready to convert her.* I had gone in to buy a battery for my watch, but she ended up selling me a new one.

What happened was a "right time" moment. God had already arranged everything perfectly. Consider all that had to align: Houston has hundreds of jewelry stores, but I chose her mom's store. Victoria could have been off that day, with another customer, or out to lunch, but she was there waiting for me.

God has similar "right times" in your future. The right people will show up, along with the healing, freedom, promotion, or the baby you're believing for. As you continue to honor God, you'll experience moments of favor where things happen that only God can orchestrate.

PROMISE:
God orders your steps, and His plan encompasses every moment of your life, from beginning to end.

Future Time

"This vision is for a future time. It describes the end, and it will be fulfilled. If it seems slow in coming, wait patiently, for it will surely take place. It will not be delayed."
HABAKKUK 2:3 (NLT)

Habakkuk said. "This vision is for a future time." It may seem slow in coming, but wait patiently, for it will surely come." Notice it doesn't say, "Maybe come." And it doesn't say, "I hope so." No, God has already set the date. The future time has already been added to your calendar. It won't be one second late.

The appointed time is the best time. As our Beginning and End, God sees the big picture of our lives; He knows what's ahead, what we'll need, and who needs to show up when. If God fulfilled everything we requested on our timetable, it could limit us. Sometimes, what we're asking for is too small.

What you're praying for may be good and a part of your destiny, but it might not be the right time yet. If there is a right time, there must also be a wrong time. If it hasn't happened yet, instead of being frustrated or worried, "God, when is my business going to grow? When am I going to meet someone?" Try a new approach. Say, "God, You know what's best for me. You see the big picture. I'm not going to live frustrated. I trust Your timing."

I know a young lady in her early thirties who had never really been in a serious relationship and was beginning to wonder if she would ever meet the right person. One day, while driving home from work, she had a flat tire and had to pull over on the side of the freeway. Almost immediately, another car pulled over, and a handsome young man stepped out. He approached her window and asked, "Can I help you?"

She took one look at him and replied, "I think you can."

He not only changed her tire but also invited her to dinner. They fell in love and got married a year and a half later. Today, they're as happy as can be, and I often see them at Lakewood Church. That wasn't a coincidence or a lucky break; it was an appointed time ordained by the Alpha and Omega.

Consider how precise God's timing was: the tire had to go flat at just the right moment. An hour later, and it wouldn't have happened. There had to be just the right amount of traffic — too many cars and he would have been late; too few, and he would have arrived early. He had to leave work at the perfect time; even a fifteen-minute delay could have disrupted everything. The timing was so exact that it fell into place down to the split second.

PROMISE:
God has already set the appointed time for your destiny or promise. Trust that He, as the Alpha and Omega, sees the complete picture of your life and knows the best time for everything to unfold. Be patient and trust His perfect timing.

Joel Osteen

My challenge to you is to trust God's timing. When you remain at rest, Almighty God will fight your battles. There are set times in your future. God sees the big picture. He knows what's best for you. He is simultaneously at the beginning and end of your life, and He knows when the right time is.

Delayed Dreams

"You intended to harm me, but God intended it all for good. He brought me to this position so I could save the lives of many people."
GENESIS 50:20 (NLT)

When Joseph was a teenager, God gave him a dream of one day being in leadership and accomplishing great things. However, his journey to that promise was far from smooth. Instead of opening doors and receiving promotions, he faced severe setbacks. His brothers, filled with jealousy, threw him into a pit. He was sold as a slave and taken to a foreign land where he didn't speak the language. Despite his hard work and integrity, he was falsely accused by his master's wife and thrown into prison.

One night, Pharaoh, the ruler of Egypt, had a perplexing dream. Someone mentioned that Joseph, the prisoner, could interpret dreams. The Scripture says, *"Pharaoh sent for Joseph at once, and he was quickly brought from the prison"* (Genesis 41:14, NLT). All those seemingly wrong events had led him to this pivotal moment. Joseph interpreted Pharaoh's dream, and Pharaoh, incredibly impressed, appointed him as the Prime Minister of Egypt, second in command only to Pharaoh himself.

Joseph later told his brothers, *"You intended to harm me, but God intended it all for good. He brought me to this position so I could save the lives of many people"* (Genesis 50:20, NLT). This reveals God's purpose in placing Joseph where he was.

Notice how all the wrongs Joseph experienced were leading to the right outcome. Without each of those wrongs, he wouldn't have reached the palace. If his brothers hadn't betrayed him, if he hadn't been sold into slavery, or if the false accusation hadn't occurred, Joseph's story would have been very different. Every setback was necessary to fulfill God's more excellent plan for his life.

The Alpha and Omega controls every aspect of your life, from start to finish. Because of your faith and patience, I believe and declare that you will experience set times of favor, healing, promotion, and breakthrough. God will fulfill the desires of your heart, and everything He has promised you will come to pass.

PROMISE:
Even in the face of setbacks, God is orchestrating every event to fulfill His greater plan for your life, bringing you into your destined position of favor and purpose, all at the right time.

Joel Osteen

Jesus, You are My Alpha and Omega

God, as the Alpha and Omega, sees the full picture of your life and has perfectly orchestrated every step according to His plan. Trust that His timing is flawless, and every challenge or delay you face is a part of His greater purpose, leading you toward the fulfillment of His promises for your life. Be patient and know that He is always working behind the scenes to bring everything to pass in the right moment.

DECLARATION PRAYER:

Heavenly Father, I come before You with faith and trust in Your perfect timing. Because of Your promises and my faithfulness, I am stepping into set times of favor, healing, promotion, and breakthrough. Lord, I believe that You are my Alpha and Omega. Your plans for me are good, and You are orchestrating every detail of my life with precision.

Even when things seem wrong or delayed, I trust You are working behind the scenes, aligning everything for my benefit. Just as You guided Joseph through betrayal and hardship to his appointed place of leadership, I know You are guiding me to the right opportunities and blessings at the correct times.

I release all frustration and worry about when things will happen, and I embrace Your timing. I declare that I will see, at the appointed time, the desires of my heart fulfilled, and Your promises come to pass.

I trust and believe that Your plans will unfold perfectly, and I will walk in the fullness of Your blessings.

In Jesus' name, amen.

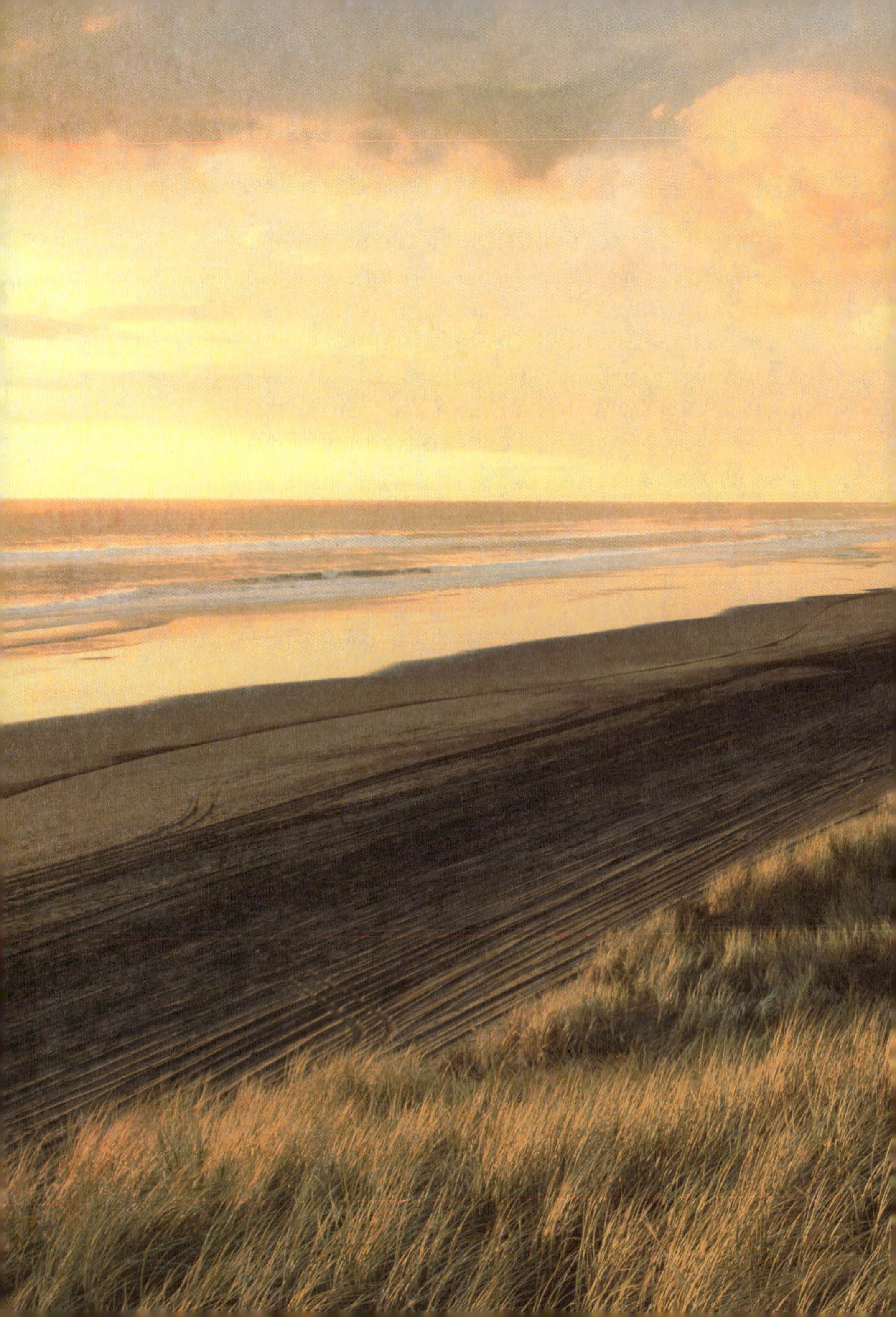

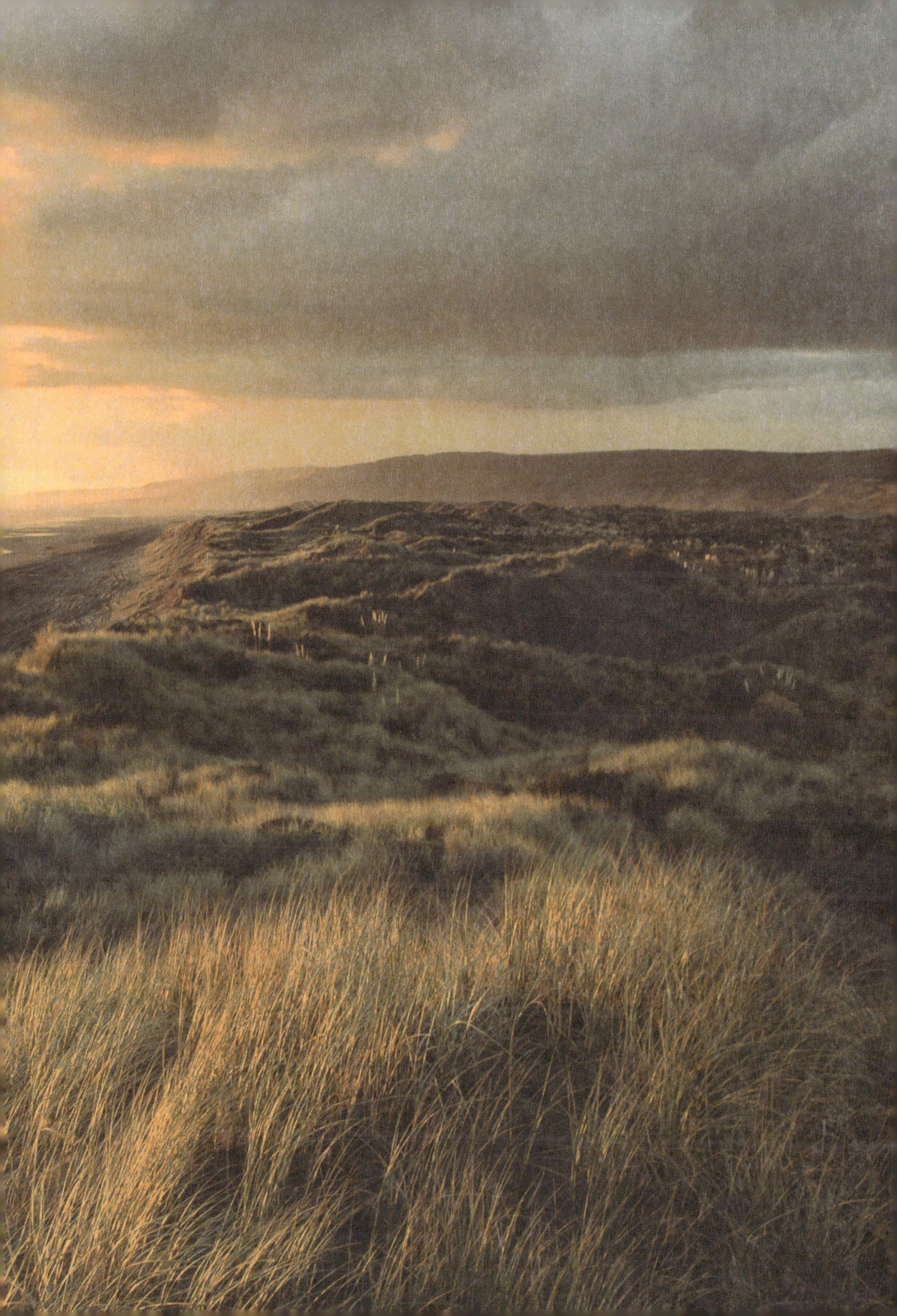

ABOUT JOEL OSTEEN MINISTRIES

Joel Osteen Ministries, rooted in Houston, Texas, is an extension of the legacy built by John and Dodie Osteen, who founded Lakewood Church in 1959. Originally meeting in a modest feed store, Lakewood has grown into one of the largest congregations in the U.S., attracting people from all walks of life. John Osteen's leadership touched millions through his television ministry, which reached over 100 countries, and his influence as a pastor's pastor. His wife, Dodie, also played a key role, especially with her testimony of miraculous healing from cancer, which has inspired countless people.

When John passed away in 1999, his son Joel stepped into leadership, despite his background in television production. Joel's transition into senior pastor marked a new era for Lakewood, with the church's global influence expanding significantly. Under Joel's leadership, Lakewood's outreach grew, broadcasting to over 200 million households, and the church became a beacon of hope for millions seeking encouragement and inspiration.

Joel's wife, Victoria, serves alongside him, contributing to the church's leadership and vision. Their daughter, Alexandra, continues the family tradition, leading worship and contributing to Lakewood Music. With a focus on uplifting messages and practical teachings, Joel Osteen Ministries aims to reach new generations, inspiring people worldwide to rise above their challenges and live their best life through faith, hope, and love.

Stay encouraged *and* inspired all through the week.

Download the Joel Osteen Daily Podcast *and* subscribe now *on* YouTube to get the latest videos.

For a full listing, visit **JoelOsteen.com/How-To-Watch**.

SiriusXM | **Apple Podcasts** | **Spotify** | **YouTube** | **Roku**

Stay connected, *be* blessed.

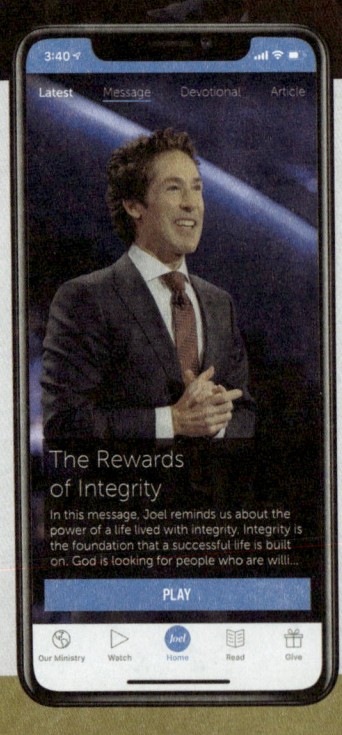

Get more from Joel & Victoria Osteen

It's time to step into the life of victory and favor that God has planned for you! Featuring new messages from Joel & Victoria Osteen, their free daily devotional, and inspiring articles, hope is always at your fingertips with the free Joel Osteen app and online at JoelOsteen.com.

Get the app and visit us today at JoelOsteen.com.

Download on the App Store

GET IT ON Google Play

CONNECT WITH US

JOEL OSTEEN MINISTRIES

m the Bread of
n the Light *I Am*
m the Resurrect
e Way, the Truth,
he *I Am* the Alpha
e Bread of Life *I A*
ght *I Am* the Goo
surrection and t
e Truth, and the L
Alpha and the